Cassell's

Intermedic... e

Multi-skills practice for ... n

Graha...

Cassell

CASSELL LTD
1 St Anne's Road, Eastbourne
East Sussex BN21 3UN

First printed 1985

ISBN 0 304 31204 5

Typesetting by CST, Eastbourne
Colour separation by Colourscan Co. Ltd, Singapore
Printed in Italy by Tipolitografia G. Canale & C. SpA, Turin

Designed by Jacky Wedgwood
Illustrations by David Armitage and Caroline Frost
Photographs by Bob Genung

Contents

Introduction

General notes

Cassell's Intermediate Short Course is a multi-skills practice course for post-Elementary students of English. It is particularly suitable for students attending short intensive courses of between two and eight weeks or part-time courses of between two and four hours a week.
The course will be of special interest to students studying in Britain or intending to visit Britain, as each unit contains a theme related to life and attitudes in Britain today.
Each unit is divided into the following sections:

- Reading
- Getting around
- Listening
- Telephoning
- Picture composition
- Discussion
- Letter-writing
- Game

An important feature of the course is its flexibility. The units need not be studied in sequence and groups may concentrate on sections of particular interest to them, such as Telephoning or Picture composition. Several sections within each unit are related thematically and many can be used independently.

Notes on the units

Cassell's Intermediate Short Course contains eight units and each unit is divided into eight sections.
The tasks and exercises have been carefully selected for their usefulness and interest.

Reading
Most reading passages are directly related to life in Britain and include topics of current concern designed to stimulate interest and discussion.

Getting around
The material included in this section is available on cassette.
Students are given opportunities to practise English in everyday situations. Suggestions for further practice are included throughout.

Listening
The material included in this section is available on cassette.
Most of the listening sections are task-based and provide opportunities for discussion.

Telephoning
The material in this section is available on cassette.
This section provides practice in telephone situations frequently encountered by visitors to Britain.

Picture composition
This section focuses on developing fluency in writing and is usually related to the topic introduced in the Reading section.

Discussion
Like the previous section, this section is usually related to the Reading topic. Topics are suitable for small group discussion and report-back.

Letter-writing
Personal and formal letter-writing styles are both introduced and practised.

Game
This section provides useful and enjoyable language practice based on various game formats, most of which will be familiar to the students.

I hope you and your students enjoy using **Cassell's Intermediate Short Course.**

For those of you who wish to refer students to books for further study, the following are recommended:

Cassell's Students' English Grammar
Cassell's Students' English Grammar Exercises with Answers (also available without answers and with separate Key)
Functional English Practice
Foundation English (and Workbooks):
- Starting English
- Discovering English
- Exploring English
- Thinking English

Acknowledgement

The author would like to thank the Editor for all her patient help and encouragement throughout the writing of this book. Without her excellent ideas and suggestions, the book would be much less interesting.

Unit One

Lacock Abbey, Wiltshire

Reading: The National Trust

1 *Read these questions:*

a What does the National Trust do?

b What types of building does it have?

c What types of land does it have?

d What problems does it have at the moment?

Hailes Abbey

National Trust for Places of Historic Interest or Natural Beauty
36 Queen Anne's Gate
London SW1H 9AS

Read the passage and answer the questions.

The National Trust is a charity which maintains beautiful places in Britain so that they are not changed by industry or new roads or building. Most are open to the public.

The National Trust has many different types of buildings. There are churches, castles and houses which have interesting or important architecture from different centuries. Other buildings are famous or interesting because of the people who lived in them, for instance the houses of Wordsworth and Sir Winston Churchill. The Trust also owns complete villages where people still live, such as Lacock in Wiltshire, which is maintained in its original state. The Trust also owns Hadrian's Wall which was built by the Romans and now lies along the border between England and Scotland.

The Trust owns land of many types including famous gardens and nature reserves where the animals, birds and fish can live in their natural surroundings. One important new idea is 'Project Neptune': the Trust is trying to buy sections of the coast of England and Wales. The Trust is afraid that the coast could be destroyed by development and that the natural beauty of the areas could be affected.

But the National Trust still has problems. The first and most obvious one is money. The cost of maintaining all the places which belong to the Trust has gone up enormously in recent years. The Trust relies on volunteers for some of its work, but has to use experts for a great deal of the maintenance.

Secondly, the Trust wants to encourage visitors but at the same time doesn't want the properties destroyed by too many visitors! A large number of visitors can cause damage. This is particularly true of the nature reserves where the birds and animals might be frightened by too many people.

If you are interested in the National Trust or want more information, contact them at the address on the left.

Getting around

1 *Listen to these conversations about the weather.*

–It's too hot to go shopping this morning!
–No, it's not. It's just pleasantly warm.
–Well, *you* go if you want to. I'll stay here and keep cool.
–OK, but it's going to be even hotter this afternoon. You won't like that!

–Oh no! It's raining again.
–Yeah, and the weather report says it's going to be cloudy and wet all day.
–I can't play football in the rain. The pitch will be too muddy.
–Well, why not stay in and help paint the ceiling?

2 *Now practise the conversations with another student.*

3 *Practise the conversations with another student, using these situations:*
cold/jogging/cool/warm/colder;
hot/sunny and hot/when it's hot/too hard/wash the car

4 *Look at this weather map for Britain. Talk about the weather with another student and make plans for the day. Imagine you are in these cities:*
Manchester, Bristol, London, Edinburgh

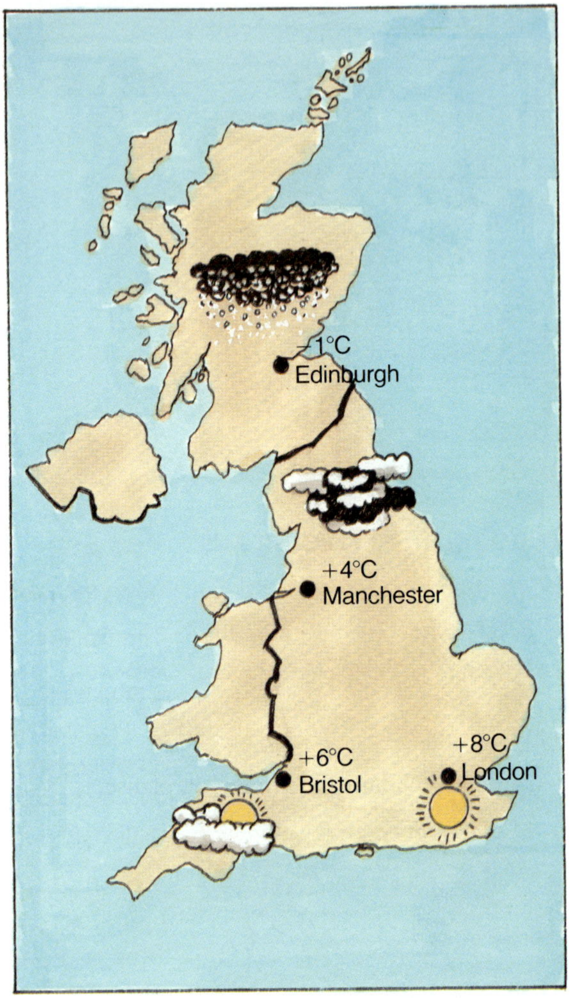

Listening

1 *Listen to the talk and write the name of the rooms on the map of the school.*

2 *Now listen again and write the special features (eg use) of each classroom next to it on the map.*

3 *Listen again and draw the arrangement of tables and chairs in each classroom.*

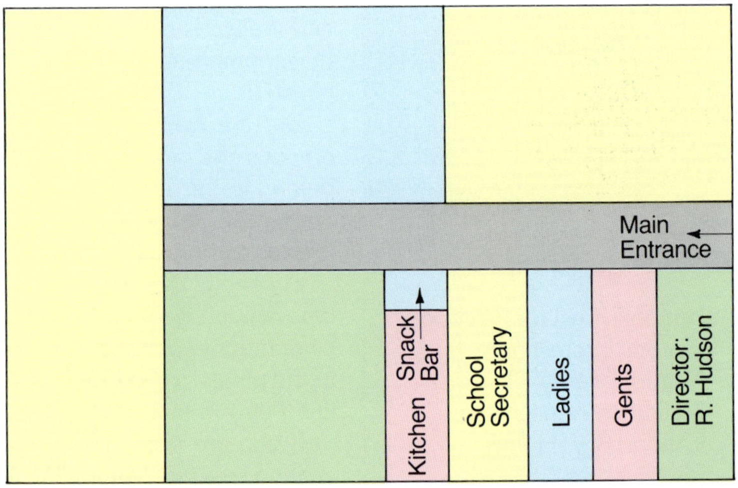

4 *Listen to the conversation and write the names of the missing buildings on the map.*

5 *Now listen again and write down a list of things that Silvia has to buy or get.*

6 *Listen again to check your answers and then draw a line to show the shortest route she can take to do everything. Compare your route with the route chosen by another student.*

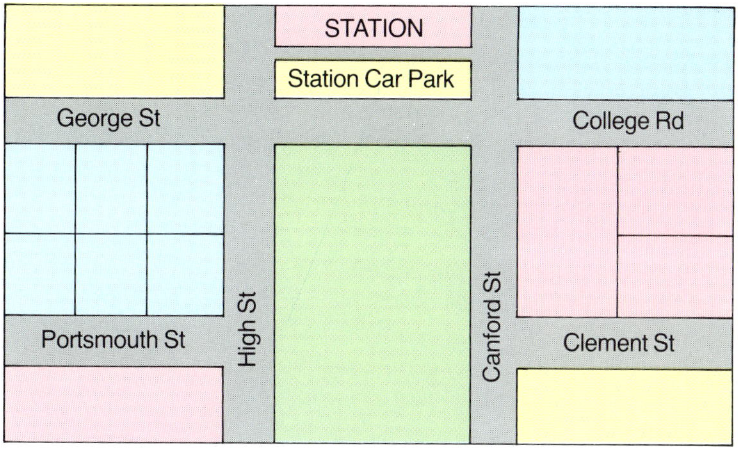

Telephoning

Getting to speak to the right person

1 *Listen to this conversation:*
– Selfenham's Department Store. Good afternoon.
– Good afternoon. I bought a camera at your store this morning and there's something wrong with it. Could you put me through to the photographic department, please?
– Certainly, madam. One moment, please.

2 *Practise the conversation with another student.*

3 *Practise the conversation with another student using:*
watch/jewellery; knives/cutlery; washing machine/service dept.

4 *Listen to this conversation:*
– Central Tourist Office. Can I help you?
– Good morning. I'd like to book a trip on the Thames, please. Do you take bookings over the phone?
– Yes, we do, sir. One moment, please. I'll put you through to our boat trips desk.

5 *Practise the conversation with another student.*

6 *Practise the conversation with another student using:*
Pearson's Bus Company/excursion to Oxford/booking clerk;
Da Luigi's/table for four/the manager.

7 *Listen to this conversation:*
– Can I speak to John, please?
– I'm sorry, but he's not here at the moment.
– Oh! When will he be back?
– I'm afraid I don't know.
– OK. Thanks a lot.

8 *Practise the conversation with another student.*

9 *Practise the conversation with another student using:*
Mary/out for a walk/about six o'clock;
Mr Robertson/gone into town/probably about five;
Christopher/out to dinner/very late, I should think.

10 *Listen to this conversation:*
– Shrivingdon College. Can I help you?
– Yes, I'd like some information about the college. Who should I speak to?
– Do you want to study here?
– Well, maybe.
– Do you know which department?
– No, not exactly.
– Hm. I'll connect you with the Registrar's Office. They should be able to give you some general information.

11 *Practise the conversation with another student using:*
British Consulate/colleges in England/study there/subject/Cultural Attaché's Office.

Picture composition

1 *Look at the pictures and answer these questions:*

a How many people do you think live in these flats?
b Do you think they are very expensive?
c Do you think there is a lot of space in them?
d Are the surroundings pleasant?
e How many families do you think live in the house?
f Do you think it is a very expensive house?
g Do you think there is a lot of space in the house?
h Are the surroundings pleasant?

2 *Now write a description of the flats and the house. Say which you would prefer to live in.*

Here are some words which may be helpful:

flat	easy to clean	roof
garden	two-storey	space
dining room	balcony	surroundings
detached house	entrance	central heating

Discussion

1 *Listen to the first part of the interview and fill in this table about voluntary service in developing countries.*

Two organisations mentioned ______
Usual age range ______
Experience necessary? ______
Skills necessary? ______
Types of work involved ______
Usual stay abroad ______
Salary ______

2 *Listen to the second part of the interview and fill in this table about the reasons for going on voluntary service.*

General wish ______
Reasons given
1 ______
2 ______
3 ______
Others? ______

3 *In groups, discuss these questions:*

a Are there similar organisations in your country?
b Do you think it is a good idea to go to a developing country as a volunteer?
c Do you think the salary is enough?
d Do you think that the usual stay is too long or too short?
e Do you think that people without skills or experience should be able to go to developing countries? What could they offer?
f Can you think of any other reasons why someone might want to go on voluntary service?

Report your answers to the whole class.

Letter-writing

1 *Read this letter and answer the questions:*

C/O 36 Eaton Court
Woodstock Road
Oxford OX2 6JH

Sat. 16th.

Dear Mum and Dad,

Just a short note to tell you that I've arrived safely. The coach was a little bit late but I finally arrived at my landlady's flat at about 7. The whole journey was quite tiring although we were well looked after all the way.

My landlady is very sweet - she had a snack ready for me when I arrived and didn't ask too many questions because she knew I was tired. She's got a pleasant flat about twenty minutes' walk from the centre of Oxford and about 10 minutes from the school. She loves flowers and plants - the flat is full of them. There's also some grass around the block of flats. Perhaps I can sunbathe there if the weather improves. Oh by the way her phone number is 52699

Oxford is a suprisingly small town. Everyone has heard of it and so everyone thinks it must be big. But it's not - there are only about 100,000 inhabitants. Basically, it's divided into two parts: the industrial area around the big car factory and the University area. The shops seem to be quite good - the town centre has everything you need. But there are tourists everywhere. I've heard many different languages since I arrived. But most tourists don't seem to stay overnight. They come for a day and then go back to London. The evenings can be fun since there are some good pubs and clubs etc.

I'll try and write again soon.

Much love
Michael

a What time did Michael arrive?
b What was the journey like?
c Does he like his landlady? Why?
d What is her flat like?
e How big is Oxford?
f What type of industry does Oxford have?
g What are the shops like?
h Do the tourists stay for a long time?

2 *Now write a letter to your parents. Include details of your arrival, where you are staying, the address and telephone number. Describe the town: Is it industrial? How big is it? Does it have any old/interesting buildings? Is there anything special or unusual about it? Are you enjoying yourself? Write the letter in the same way as Michael's letter.*

Game

1 *Work with another student. Cover up one of these two pictures. Get the other student to cover up the other picture. Now describe your picture to the other student. Let him/her describe his/her picture to you. What are the differences?*

2 *Now do the same with these town plans.*

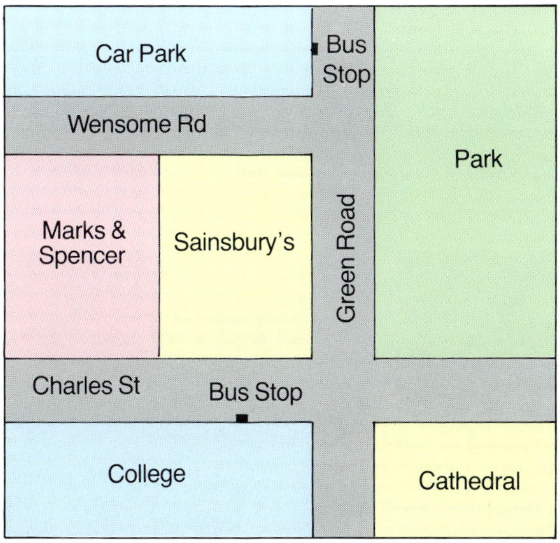

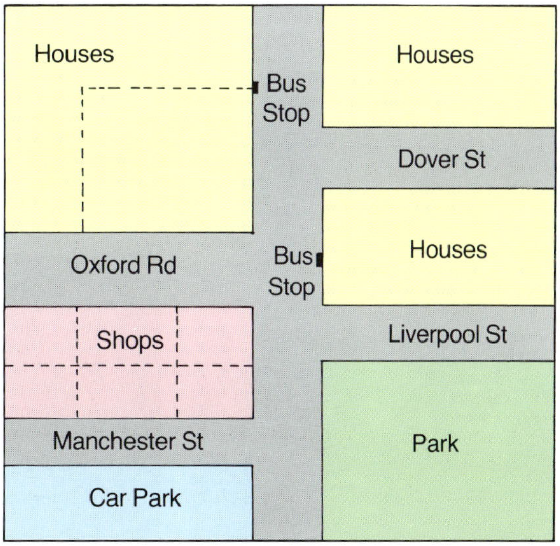

Unit Two

Reading: Minorities in Britain

Read the passage and then fill in the table with the information required.

People from many different countries have come to live in Britain. They have come to Britain for a lot of different reasons and at different periods in Britain's history. Three of the main groups are described here.

Firstly, in the mid-fifties (i.e. around 1955) there was a great deal of immigration from the West Indies when there was a labour shortage in Britain. Most West Indians left their islands because they felt they could get a secure job in Britain with a higher standard of living.

The second group of immigrants came in the early sixties. They were mainly from Pakistan, India and what is now Bangladesh. They also came because of a labour shortage in Britain and because of the prospect of a higher standard of living. They went to the cities in the Midlands and North where the labour shortage was greatest.

The third group arrived in the mid-seventies for completely different reasons. These were the Ugandan Asians who were allowed into Britain because they had been forced out of Uganda. Most of them were British passport holders. But at that time there was no labour shortage in Britain and there was a lot of protest over their arrival. The first two groups came to jobs. The Ugandan Asians arrived at a time of high unemployment and a housing shortage.

	West Indians	Asians	Ugandan Asians
Arrival			
Conditions in home country			
Reasons for coming			

Getting around

1 *Listen to this conversation:*

– Good morning sir.
– Good morning. I'd like to hire a bicycle.
– Certainly, sir. What sort of trips are you going to use it for?
– I'm — er — not quite sure. What do you mean?
– Well, are you going to use it for short trips around town or are you going to make longer journeys into the countryside?
– Oh, both really.
– Right, sir. Then I recommend this Luxus Grand Tourer. It's got 10 speeds, it's fully equipped with everything and only costs £12 a week to hire, plus a £25 deposit.

2 *Practise the conversation with another student.*

3 *Practise the conversation with another student using this information:*

a boat/around Oxford/up the river/Maxipower 200/big engine/£200 a week/£400 deposit.

b tent/to the hills/up the mountains/Everest Superheat/comes with sleeping-bags/£50 a week/£100.

Listening

1 *Listen to the recording and fill in the answers:*

Came from ______________ *Date of arrival* ______________
Now living in ______________ *Profession* ______________
Reason for coming ______________
Advantages of living in Britain ______________
Disadvantages of living in Britain ______________

2 *Listen to the recording and fill in the answers:*

Came from ______________ *Date of arrival* ______________
Now living in ______________ *Profession* ______________
Reason for coming ______________
Advantages of living in Britain ______________
Disadvantages of living in Britain ______________

Telephoning

1 *Listen to the telephone conversation. Write the message on the message pad:*

– Good morning. Could I speak to Jane, please?
– I'm sorry. She's away for the day.
– Oh, do you know what time she'll be back?
– Well, she said she'd be back some time this evening, but I don't know exactly when.
– OK. Could I leave a message, please?
– Yes, sure. Hang on a sec while I get a pencil . . . OK.
– Could you tell her that Jimmy called. Could she please call me back. Either this evening before ten or tomorrow morning after nine. My number is 01-229-2249.
– OK, got it. Before ten tonight or after nine tomorrow, number 01-229-2249.
– That's right. Thanks a lot.
– Not at all.

Message for: __________

from: __________

Message: __________

Number: __________

2 *Now act out the telephone conversation with another student using your message notes.*

3 *Listen to the telephone conversation. Write the message on the message pad:*

– Turner Travel. Good morning.
– Good morning. Could I speak to Mr Richardson, please?
– I'm afraid he's not in the office this morning. Can I take a message?
– Oh, will he be back this afternoon?
– Yes, he will be. Can I get him to call you?
– Yes, please. My name is Maria Gonzalez and my number is Eastbourne 20899. I'll be here until about half past five.
– Maria Gonzalez Eastbourne 20899, and you'll be there until five-thirty. Can Mr Richardson reach you tomorrow at the same number?
– Yes, any time after half past nine.
– OK, Ms Gonzalez, I'll make sure he gets the message. Thank you for calling.
– Thank you, goodbye.

Message for: __________

from: __________

Message: __________

Number: __________

4 *Now act out the telephone conversation with another student using your message notes.*

Picture composition

Look at the pictures on page 15.

Answer these questions about each picture.

1 Who is he/she?
2 Where is he/she?
3 Why do you think he/she is unhappy?
4 Would he/she be happy in your country?
5 Why/why not?

Discussion

1 *Answer these questions:*

a What was George's decision when he finished university?
b What were his reasons?
c Do you think he is happy in Britain? Give reasons.

George was born in Greece in 1946. When he was 18, his mother's sister offered to finance his education in Britain. A year later he arrived in Nottingham to attend college to do his 'A' levels. He passed these successfully and went on to Nottingham University, where he studied Economics and Administration.

After his degree he was faced with a big decision: should he go back to Greece or try for a job in Britain? He had studied hard, so finding a job in Britain probably would not be too difficult. He felt that he had lost contact with Greece and his Greek friends after five years in Britain. His friends were now mostly British and he was happy in Britain. There were plenty of things which he didn't like, but he felt that it would be too big a change again to return to Greece.

He applied for a job with a large engineering company who were advertising for a post in their administration department. He got the job and has been with them ever since. Now he has applied for British citizenship. He feels that he was right to stay in Britain, even though he had to renew his work permit every year. Now that problem is solved. He still likes to visit Greece, but his home is in Britain.

2 *Answer these questions:*

a What does Chuck feel about living in England?
b What was life like in New York?
c Why will he eventually return to the United States?

Chuck was born in the United States and lived there until he was 42. Then he gave up his job and moved to England. There are not so many pressures at work, and life is more gentle in England. In New York, he had to be at work at eight o'clock every morning and finished at five-thirty, with just half an hour for lunch. It was hard work all day in the office. And then he had to travel for an hour each morning and evening just to get home.

But he takes home a lower salary than he did in the United States. This means that he doesn't have so much money to spend. He feels that this is OK for the moment, but eventually he'll go back to the States. He regards living in England as a long holiday; he's earning enough money to live reasonably for two years and he's enjoying himself and relaxing. But he realises that it cannot last for ever. His home is really the United States and that's where most of his friends are.

Groupwork

3 *Discuss these questions in groups and then report back to the class.*

a Make a table of the advantages and disadvantages of living in England.

b Make a table of countries you would like to live in and the reasons.

c Are there any groups of people from other countries in your country? Why did they come to your country?

Letter-writing

1 *Look at the conversation in Getting around. Then read this letter.*
The letter was written to the bicycle company after the man returned the bicycle.

a *Make a list of the things the assistant said.*
b *Make a list of the things which were not true.*
c *Make a list of the things which were not explained properly.*

34 Jermyn Street,
Brighton,
E. Sussex BN5 2AH
26/8/85

The Manager
Tourfree Bicycle Hire
26, Mersham Gardens
Cambridge CB2 1DH

Dear Sir/Madam,

Ref: Bicycle hire between 22nd August and 25th August 1985

Last week I hired a bicycle from your company which I returned yesterday. I would like to complain about the condition of the bicycle.

Your assistant said that it had ten speeds but there were only three. Your assistant said that it was well equipped. But the light did not work properly and the bell did not work at all. Your assistant did not tell me that the cost of hiring did not include tax. Your assistant told me when I returned the bicycle that my deposit would be returned in a week. Because I am leaving Britain in four days this is unacceptable.

I would therefore like a refund of at least some of the cost of hiring the bicycle and my deposit within the next four days.

Yours faithfully,

Carlos J da Souza

2 *Now look at the third conversation in Getting around ('Tent').*

a *Make a list of the things the assistant would have said.*
b *Make a list of the things which might have gone wrong.*
c *Make a list of the things which might not have been explained properly.*

3 *Write a letter to the tent-hire company like the one above. Complain about the things which were wrong with the tent. Complain about the things which were not explained properly. Ask for a refund.*

Game

Groupwork

Look at the pictures. Make a list of all the things you can see in each picture.

Which things in the picture tell you about his/her job?

Everything in the picture is important.

Give reasons for choosing a particular job.

Unit Three

Reading: Secondary school education

Here are two extracts from typical letters sent to students and their parents by schools when the students have completed their tenth year at school. 'O' level exams are taken the following year, while 'A' levels are taken at about the age of 18. At the age of 16, an alternative to 'O' levels is the Certificate of Secondary Education (CSE), which is normally taken by less academic students.

CHOICE OF SUBJECTS FOR''O' LEVELS

COMPULSORY: English; Maths.
SCIENCES (You must take at least one): Physics, Chemistry, Biology.
ARTS (You must take at least one): History, Geography, Art, Music, French, Spanish.
HUMANITIES (You must take at least one): Economics, Sociology.

Choose two or more from the above list or from:
Computer Studies, Technical Drawing, Statistics, German, English Literature.
More subjects may be offered if there is sufficient demand.
Please talk to your form teacher about it.

CHOICE OF SUBJECTS FOR 'A' LEVELS.

Choose either three or two subjects.

Possible combinations:
Maths,Physics,Chemistry.
Physics,Chemistry,Biology.

English,History,Geography.
English,History,French.
Pure Maths,Applied Maths,Economics.
Pure Maths,Applied Maths, Computer Studies.
History,Economics, Sociology.

Other combinations may be possible. This will depend on the timetable and the number of students who wish to do that particular combination. Please see your form teacher about your preferred combination.

We talked to an ex-teacher who is now in business about the subjects offered at 'O' and 'A' level. He suggested that the courses up to 'O' level provided a fairly good general basic education. There was a sufficient range of subjects, but smaller schools, eg those in rural communities, were not able to offer everything. He felt that the courses for 'A' levels were far too specialised. Only three subjects were studied. This was too narrow. Students did not get a general education after the age of 16. He also thought that most technical subjects were excluded from 'A' levels and that these exams were not practical enough. Some of the individual 'A' level subjects were quite interesting, but others were simply academic study. He felt it would be better to study five or six subjects more generally.

Answer these questions:

1 Which 'O' levels does everyone have to do?
2 How many 'O' levels seem to be recommended as a maximum?
3 Could you study French, German and Spanish 'O' levels at the same time?
4 What 'A' levels would you do if you wanted to become an engineer?
5 Is it possible to study English, Maths and Sociology at 'A' level?
6 What did the ex-teacher feel about the 'O' level courses?
7 Make a list of his criticisms of the 'A' levels.
8 What did he suggest as an alternative?

Getting around

1 *Listen to this conversation:*

– Hey, Mary, I need some help.
– OK, coming.
– I've got to get this jacket cleaned. Is there a dry cleaners near here?
– Yes, there's one on North Parade.
– Oh, yes, I know. Do you think they do repairs as well?
– Hmm. I don't know. But you could ask them.
– Yeah, I'll try.

2 *Now listen to this conversation:*

– Good morning, sir.
– Good morning. I'd like this jacket cleaned, please.
– Yes, sir.
– And do you do repairs?
– I'm afraid not, sir. You'll have to go to a tailor's.
– Oh, OK.
– This jacket will be ready on Thursday, sir. Here's your ticket.
– Thanks, goodbye.
– Goodbye.

3 *Practise the conversations with another student.*

4 *Practise again using:* dress/coat/trousers.

5 *Imagine you want to buy some cassettes and have your cassette headphones repaired. Make up two conversations like the ones above and then practise them with another student.*

Listening

1 *Listen to the conversation, in stages if necessary. Fill in the table.*

What to do	Advantages	Disadvantages
Stay at school		
Further education college		
Youth Training Scheme		

2 *Listen to the conversation, in stages if necessary. Answer the questions:*

a Who is talking?
b What is the disadvantage of university?
c What are the advantages of doing a sandwich course?
d Are there any disadvantages in doing a sandwich course?
e What do you think John will do? Why?

Telephoning

1 *Listen to John and Mary's conversation.*

– Eastbourne 43691.
– Hi, John, this is Mary. I got your message to call you.
– Hello, Mary. At last! I've been trying to reach you for days.
– Right. How about meeting for a drink?
– Great.
– OK. Well, what about tomorrow?
– I'm afraid I can't. I've promised to visit Jane in hospital. How about Friday?
– That's fine. Where shall we meet?
– How about the Blue Boar? It's fairly comfortable and not too crowded.
– OK. What time?
– About 8.30?
– Umm, I'd prefer 9 o'clock or after. It gives me a chance to do some things at home first.
– OK. Let's say quarter past nine.
– Right, I'll see you on Friday at 9.15 in the Blue Boar.
– Great. See you then.
– See you.

a When are they going to meet?
b Where are they going to meet?

2 *Listen to their conversation again.*

a Why can't John go out tomorrow?
b Why does he suggest the Blue Boar?
c Why does Mary prefer the later time?

3 *Listen to their conversation again.*

a How does Mary suggest the day they should meet?
b How does John suggest the day they should meet?

4 *Practise the conversation with another student.*

5 *Practise the conversation with another student. Make up your own reasons and times.*

6 *Listen to Mr Richardson's conversation with Ms Gonzalez.*

– Eastbourne 20899.
– Is that Ms Gonzalez?
– Yes, speaking.
– Good morning, this is Mr Richardson from Turner Travel. You asked me to call you.
– Oh yes, Mr Richardson, thank you for calling back. Are my travel documents ready yet?
– One moment please . . . Yes, tickets, hotel reservations and car hire — all confirmed.
– Fine. When can I collect them?
– Whenever you like. We close this afternoon at 5.30.
– Oh, I don't think I'll be able to make it by then. What time do you open tomorrow morning?
– At 9.30.
– Um. And are you closed at lunchtime tomorrow?
– No, we're open right through lunchtime.
– Fine, I'll be in at about one o'clock.
– OK. Everything will be ready for you.
– Thank you very much. Bye.
– Bye.

a What has Mr Richardson got ready for Ms Gonzalez?
b When can she collect them?

7 *Listen to their conversation again.*

a Why does he call her?
b Was she able to collect the documents that afternoon?
c Will she collect them tomorrow morning?

8 *Listen to their conversation again and write down Maria's questions.*

9 *Practise the conversation with another student.*

10 *Practise the conversation with another student, using your own information and times.*

Picture composition

Look at the words under the pictures. They may help you talk about the things you see.

Answer these questions:

1 What is the name of the bank cashier?
2 Why do you think he went to evening classes?
3 Do you think it was difficult for him to go to evening classes?
4 Why do you think he applied for the new job?

Pairwork

Talk about each picture alternately with another student. Help one another if necessary.

Writing

Write the story of the pictures. Use your answers to the questions given above. Begin: David Jones was a cashier in a bank but found the job very boring . . .

cashier/bored

suggest/study

pass exam

receive certificate

advertisement

CV/application

interview

successful/Junior Partner

Discussion

Advertisement

Wanted:
Secretary/Personal Assistant

A Secretary/Personal Assistant is required for an office which deals with international business.
The candidate must have office experience in a similar position, an excellent telephone voice and manner, good shorthand and typing.

Good salary.
Applications in writing with a full c.v. to

Bluestone International
Candley House
Cantrovile St.
London EC3T 6LJ.

1 *Look at this advertisement for a secretary and discuss in groups:*

a What qualifications are required?
b What experience is required?
c What sort of personality should the person have?

2 You are the personnel manager of the company. You have received the following 3 CVs. *Which one is the most appropriate and why?*

Discuss in groups.

1

NAME: Charterhouse, Janet
DATE OF BIRTH: 6.5.56
MARITAL STATUS: single
EDUCATION: Little Ilford Comprehensive School.
'O' levels: English, Maths, Geography, History, French.
Ilford Secretarial College:
RSA Shorthand and Typing Grades: 80/55.
EMPLOYMENT RECORD:
June 1975 – Oct 1976: Temporary Secretary with Ilford Girls (name and address supplied) Attachments to various companies.
Jan 1977 – date: Secretary to the Personnel Manager, Thomas Foulkes & Co., Biscuit Manufacturers.
REASON FOR APPLICATION: Present Company moving out of London. Wishes to remain in East London.

2

NAME: DUTOIT Doris
DATE OF BIRTH: 23.4.58
MARITAL STATUS: married
EDUCATION: Stratford Girls Comprehensive
'O' Levels: English, Maths, History, French, Spanish.
North-East London Polytechnic
Secretarial French and Spanish.
RSA Shorthand and typing Grades: 70/45
EMPLOYMENT RECORD:
Aug. 1978 - Apr. 1980: Secretary to the Manager, Expo-International Paris.
Apr. 1980 - date: Housewife
REASON FOR APPLICATION: Wishes to re-enter employment. Husband has moved to UK.

3

NAME: Easton, Charlene
DATE OF BIRTH: 22/8/54
MARITAL STATUS: married
EDUCATION: Moss Side Comprehensive, Manchester
'O' Levels: English, Maths
Abraham Moss College, Manchester
RSA Shorthand and Typing Grades 80/55
EMPLOYMENT RECORD:
Aug 1973 – Sept 1978: Secretary to the Sales Director, Watson's Brewery, Manchester.
Jan 1979 – Dec 1979: Secretary (Grade H), Department of Employment, Stratford E11.
Jan 1980 – Dec 1982: Secretary (Typing Pool), Persuasive Advertising Ltd, East Ham, E13
Jan 1983 – : Unemployed.
REASON FOR APPLICATION: unemployed, wish to re-enter employment.

Letter-writing

Read this letter and fill in the table.

29 Orchard Way,
Hillingstone,
Kent CT34 6TH

28/7/85

Dear Mary,

Thanks so much for your call last night. It was really great to talk to you again. It's good to know that you're well and I'll hear all the details when you arrive.

I talked to John after you phoned and we feel that the best weekend would be three weeks from now (i.e. the weekend of Saturday 19th. Aug.) I'm afraid the next two weekends are rather busy since John's mother is going into hospital.. We'll be visiting her quite a lot.

We can go on some lovely walks (if it doesn't rain!!) and there's a good play on at Canterbury theatre that weekend. I'll try and get some tickets soon.

So, how about that weekend? I hope you don't mind the change in plan. I hope you can make it then.

Much love
Jean

Suggested weekend ____________________

Reasons why not before ____________________

Reasons for that weekend ____________________

Read the first letter again and then write a letter to your friend saying when you could visit London using the following information:

Write four paragraphs.

Para 1: Thank your friend for the phone call.
Para 2: Suggest Saturday as a change of plan/ give reasons for not Friday.
Para 3: Give reasons for coming Saturday.
Para 4: Say that you hope this is OK.

Game

In groups, look at these photographs. What are they?

Make suggestions to other members of your group.

Say things like:

It could be . . .

They could be . . .

As a group, decide what they are.

The group with the most correct answers wins the game.

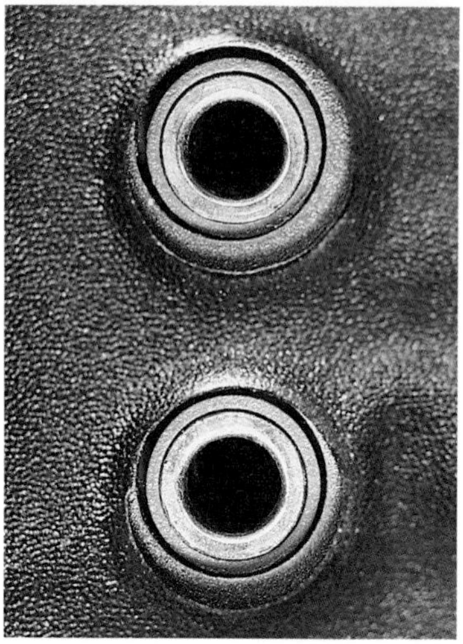

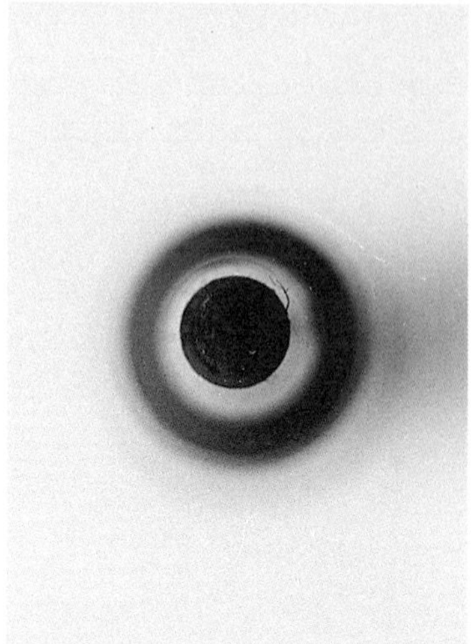

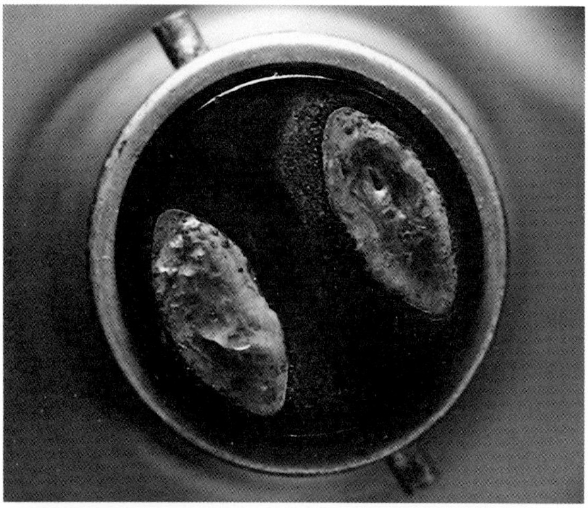

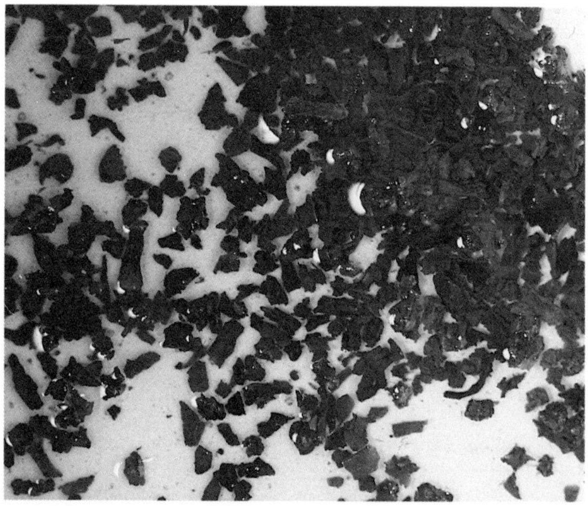

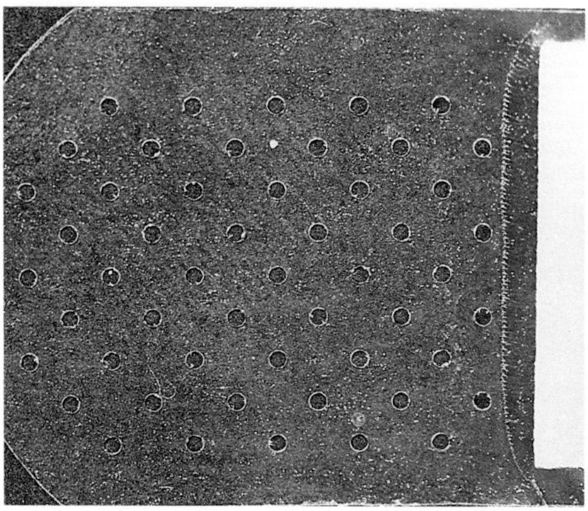

Unit Four

Reading: Television

1 *Look at the list of programmes for BBC1 and for ITV.*

Fill in the chart below about the programmes. Use your dictionary to find out what the words in the left-hand column mean.

2 *You may find that certain programmes occur under two types!*

What are they?

BBC1

7.40 **Get Set Go!** Michael Barrymore presents another edition of the fast-moving word game.
8.10 **Panorama: The Battle for Power.** A report on the government's plans to keep power stations working despite the continuing miners' strike.
9.00 **News** with John Humphrys.
9.25 **Film: Escape** (1980) starring Timothy Bottoms. The first showing on British television for this thriller, based on fact, about a young American's attempt to be the first prisoner to escape from the Lecumberri Prison in Mexico since Pancho Villa decamped in 1913. Directed by Robert Lewis.
11.00 **Film 84.** Barry Norman with news and reviews of, among others, 1984, The Woman in Red and A Private Function, the location report film.
11.28 **News** headlines.
11.30 **Sparks.** Details of ambitious youngsters' enterprises (r).
11.55 **Weather.**

The Times
Monday, 15th October 1984

ITV

7.00 **The Krypton Factor.** The Third semifinal of the brain and brawn competition (Oracle).
7.30 **Coronation Street.** Jack Duckworth lives to regret the day wife Vera finds him a job (Oracle).
8.00 **Tripper's Day.** The late Leonard Rossiter stars as the harassed Norman Tripper, manager of a supermarket, this week trying to cope with a flooded storeroom.
8.30 **World in Action: The Coal Warriors.** An examination of an episode from the life of both Arthur Scargill and Ian MacGregor which, it is believed, was the basis for their beliefs today. Arthur Scargill's was a mass picket at Slatley coal depot, Birmingham, in 1972; Ian MacGregor's was a pit strike in Gilette, Wyoming, when he was chairman of Amex.
9.00 **Quincy.** The pathologist investigates the death by drowning of a college student.
10.00 **News at Ten** followed by Thames news headlines.
10.30 **Hammer House of Mystery and Suspense: The Corvini Inheritance.** A neighbour helps a woman who complains she is being menaced by a peeping tom. Starring Jan Francis and David McCallum.
11.55 **The Bounder.** Comedy series starring Peter Bowles and George Cole (r).
12.25 **Night Thoughts.**

Type of programme	Number on BBC1	Number on ITV
News		
Documentaries		
Competitions/quizzes		
Comedies		
Serials		
Series		

Getting around

1 *Listen to this conversation:*

– Good morning, sir.
– Good morning. I've come to enquire about coach excursions. What is available on Saturday?
– Well, there's a very good trip to Stratford-on-Avon, sir. It includes a tour of the town and tickets for the theatre in the evening.
– Hm, that sounds good. What else is there?
– There's also a trip to Cambridge with a tour of the colleges.
– Fine, thanks. When do I need to book?
– Well . . . as soon as possible, really. But Thursday ought to be OK.
– Great, thanks. I'll come in tomorrow.
– Thanks, bye.

2 *Practise the conversation with another student.*

3 *Practise the conversation with another student using this information:*

Boat trips:
1 Richmond and Hampton Court. Tour of Hampton Court.
2 Greenwich and National Maritime Museum. Tour of National Maritime Museum.

Listening

Listen to each speaker and make a list of the things they like about television programmes.

Make a list of the things they don't like and a list of changes (if any) they would like to see.

1

Likes ______________________________

____

Dislikes ______________________________

____

Changes ______________________________

____

2

Likes ______________________________

____

Dislikes ______________________________

____

Changes ______________________________

____

Telephoning

Listen to these telephone conversations and write down the travel details.

– Turner Travel, good morning.
– Good morning. Could you give me information about lunchtime flights to Lisbon from London, please?
– Certainly, sir. One moment, please . . . Well, sir, there's a British Airways flight at 14.30 arriving at 16.05.
– British Airways, departing at 14.30, arriving 16.05. What's the flight number?
– That's BA434. And there's a TAP flight leaving at 14.50, arriving at 16.20. Flight number TP451.
– TAP, departing at 14.50, arriving at 16.20, flight number TP451. Thanks. I'll call back later with a definite booking.

– British Rail, good morning.
– Good morning. Could you give me the train times for Oxford to London at about 5.30 in the evening?
– Certainly, sir. There's a train at 5.20. You have to change at Reading and you arrive in London at 6.26.
– 5.20, change at Reading, arrive 6.26.
– Or there's a train at 5.30 which is direct to London. Arriving 6.30.
– 5.30 direct to London arriving 6.30. Good. Thanks a lot.
– Not at all. Bye.

London dep. ____________________
Lisbon arr. ____________________
Airline ____________________
Flight No. ____________________

Oxford dep. ____________________
Change ____________________
London arr. ____________________

Picture composition

1 *Look at these pictures and answer the following questions about each one:*

a What type of television programme is this?
b Do you have many of these programmes in your country?
c Do you like this type of programme?
d Do you think that more of these programmes should be shown or fewer?

2 *Now choose one of the four types of programme and write a paragraph saying whether you think there are enough/too many of these programmes in your country. Say why you like or dislike them.*

Start like this:
On . . . television we have . . . hours of . . .

You might also want to use:
I like this type of programme because . . .
I think there should be more/fewer . . .

3 *Now choose another type of programme — one that is not shown above. Write a similar paragraph about these programmes in your country.*

Discussion

Here are the headlines from the day's news:

Famine continues in Africa
Airplane hijack in Miami
Autobahn accident in Germany, 15 killed
French student protest
Strike at car factory in Liverpool
Chancellor of Exchequer raises VAT 1%
US Govt reports continued growth of US economy
Gatwick airport to be enlarged?
Chinese leaders decide to reform Chinese industry – more competition
Nuclear peace campaigners march in London
Lost lion found
More oil under North Sea?
New sausage record
EEC discusses more money for UK

Your group has to produce a televison news programme lasting 20 minutes.

Your task is to read the headlines and decide which reports you would use.

In your group, divide the headlines into the following categories: (NB one headline may go into more than one category).

Headlines which are:
– new/about events that have not happened before
– important for many people
– concerned with disasters
– concerned with future plans
– possibly funny.

Now discuss these questions within your group.

Which type of news is most important?
How many stories can be presented well in twenty minutes?
Should there be one or two 'big' stories and five or six 'smaller' stories?

Present your news programme to the class and give reasons why you chose the particular headlines.

Letter-writing

Read this letter:

Dear Jean,

Many thanks for your letter. It would be great to see you and I'd love to see Charles again. It's really kind of you to invite me to stay with you both.

Unfortunately, I can't manage the weekend you suggest. I have a dinner invitation for the Saturday night which I've already accepted. Would it be possible to come and see you a fortnight later? I hope this fits in with your plans. Please do let me know if it's inconvenient.

Much love

Mary

1 *Fill in this table about the letter:*

Reason for change of plan ____________________

____

Suggested time ____________________

2

Read the letter you wrote in the last Unit. Imagine you have to reply to it using the information in this table. Write the reply in two paragraphs:

Para 1: Thank your friend for the letter. Say it would be good to see him/her.

Para 2: Say that you can't come on the day suggested. Give reasons and make another suggestion.

Reason for change of plan

extra class practice on Saturday afternoon.

Suggested day following Saturday.

Read this letter:

Dr. D.W. Smith, 24, Sixton Rd., Cambridge

Dear Ms Jones, 23.9.85

Dr Smith is unable to see you next Tuesday (29th) because he is attending a conference in London.
Would you like an appointment with one of the other doctors on the same day? Or would you prefer to see Dr Smith on a later date?
He will be back in the surgery on Friday 1st October.
Perhaps you would telephone to make a new appointment.
Please accept my apologies for this inconvenience.

Yours faithfully

M. Warburton

M Warburton
(Secretary)

3 *Fill in this table about the letter:*

Reason for cancelling appointment ____________

____

Alternative possibilities ____________

4 *Look at this table:*

Reason for preferring Dr Smith

own regular doctor

Alternative times/days

from Mon 4th Oct/afternoons

Reason for writing

surgery telephone always engaged

5 *Write a formal reply to the letter from Ms Warburton. Write three paragraphs:*

Para 1: Thank her for the letter.
Para 2: Give reason for preferring Dr Smith; state when available.
Para 3: Say you have tried to telephone but unsuccessfully.

Game

1 Here are some anagrams of TV programmes.

Try to find the titles.
Check them with the Reading section on page 25.

a

eggs tote (3 words)
where at (1 word)
skraps (1 word)
neat wents (3 words)
yes, drip part (2 words)
he boned rut (2 words)

b

And here are some famous American TV series:
all sad (1 word)
a baz non (1 word)
gum man (1 word)

c

And, finally, how is your knowledge of English literature?
the lam (1 word) (a play)
sword throw (1 word) (a poet)
a ram in flam (2 words) (a novel)

2 *Make anagrams of some current film titles.*

Unit Five

Reading: Fitness and diet

Each day, the average British man or woman eats about 400 calories in the form of sugar. It is eaten in many different ways: in fruit, in biscuits and cakes, in sweets and desserts and in coffee and tea. But is this sugar good for you?

Sugar (both brown and white) has been extracted from sugar cane or from sugar beet.

Some people say that sugar gives you energy, but this is not true. Your liver holds enough sugar for you to run a marathon! If you consume sugar, the body absorbs it quickly and stores it as fat. Within an hour or two the sugar-eater often feels more tired and hungry than before. It is 'false' energy. Sugar-eating is probably a habit — like smoking. Some sugar is necessary. It is best in the form of fruit. The sugar in fruit is absorbed slowly in the body and is not stored as fat.

Give up sugar!

1 Give up sugar in tea and coffee. If this is difficult, begin by replacing it with sweeteners. But sweeteners may be harmful to you. So try to give up sugar completely.

2 Choose mineral water or tap water instead of soft drinks (eg Coca-Cola or 7-Up). Add water to unsweetened fruit juice because it still contains too much sugar. This reduces the amount of sugar in each drink. If you're drinking gin and tonic, use 'diet' tonic.

3 Eat fresh fruit instead of sweets and desserts after dinner. Fresh fruit has much less sugar than biscuits, cakes and desserts. The sugar in fresh fruit is absorbed slowly in the body, so you don't feel hungry so quickly.

1 *Answer these questions:*

a How much sugar does the average British person eat per day?
b How do we eat sugar?
c Where does brown sugar come from?
d What happens when you eat sugar?
e What is the best way to get sugar into the body?

2 *Fill in this table with the things you should not do (old habits) and the things you should do (new habits):*

Old habits	New habits
coffee/tea with sugar	without sugar

Getting around

1 *Listen to this conversation:*

– Well, what sort of restaurant shall we go to?
– I like that vegetarian place on Broad Street.
– Oh! Do they serve meat as well?
– I don't think so.
– Well, how about the Casa Mia? They serve both meat and vegetarian food.
– How expensive is it there?
– Not too bad. Probably about £6 each plus drinks.
– OK. Let's go there.

2 *Practise the conversation with another student.*

3 *Practise the conversation with another student using this information:*

Indian restaurant on the High Street/English food?/Indian restaurant on George St/English and Indian/£7.

4 *Listen to this conversation:*

– Well, what sort of snack do you want?
– Oh, just some chips will do.
– Chips? You're supposed to be on a diet! You should have a salad or something like that.
– I know I should. I know. OK, let's have salad sandwiches, then.
– Umm. That sounds better.
– There's a salad bar just round the corner.
– OK. Let's go there.

5 *Practise the conversation with another student.*

6 *Practise the conversation with another student using this information:*
a cream cake/a cream cake?/a yoghurt/a café.

Listening

1 *Listen to the discussion in the doctor's surgery. Take notes of what the doctor advises the patient to do.*

2 *Listen to the couple's conversation. Make a list of the woman's suggestions about dieting.*

Telephoning

1 *Listen to the first conversation. Write down the name, address and telephone number.*

– Directory Enquiries. Which town, please?
– Er, York, please.
– York. And what's the name, please?
– Cooke, with an 'e' at the end.
– Do you have an initial, please?
– Yes, G, D.
– And an address?
– Umm, 14, Belsize Crescent.
– Thank you, sir. The number is York 22019.
– York 22019. Thank you. Goodbye.
– Bye.

2 *Practise the conversation with another student.*

3 *Practise the conversation with another student using your own information.*

4 *Listen to the second conversation.* Why can't the *Directory Enquiries* operator give the information required?

– Directory Enquiries. Which town, please?
– London, please.
– London. And what's the name, please?
– Brown.
– Do you have an initial, please?
– Yes, J.
– And an address, please?
– I'm afraid not.
– I'm afraid I can't help you, madam. You see, we have three pages of 'J Brown' in London and it would take you a long time to phone them all!
– Oh yes . . . Oh well, I'll try asking some friends. Thank you for trying. Goodbye.
– Goodbye, madam.

5 *Practise the conversation with another student.*

6 *Practise the conversation with another student using another familiar English name (e.g. Smith).*

7 *Listen to the third conversation.* Why doesn't the *Directory Enquiries* operator give the caller a number?

– Directory Enquiries, which town, please?
– Exeter, please.
– And the name, please?
– Anderson.
– Do you have an initial, please?
– Yes, J, S.
– And an address?
– Erm, 29 Greenwood Avenue.
– Thank you, madam . . . I'm afraid we don't have a 'J S Anderson' with that address listed. He or she may be ex-directory. Would you like me to find out?
– Well, I'm certain of the address, so they must be ex-directory. No, it's okay. I'll drop them a line instead. Thank you for your help.
– Not at all. Goodbye.
– Goodbye.

8 *Practise the conversation with another student.*

9 *Practise the conversation with another student using your own information.*

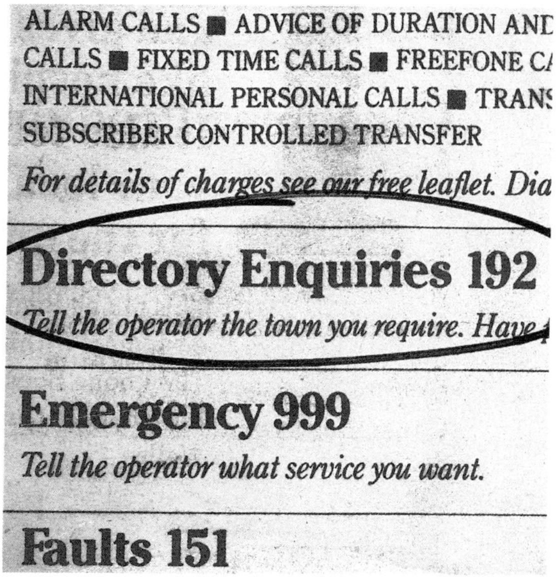
ALARM CALLS ■ ADVICE OF DURATION AND
CALLS ■ FIXED TIME CALLS ■ FREEFONE C
INTERNATIONAL PERSONAL CALLS ■ TRANS
SUBSCRIBER CONTROLLED TRANSFER
For details of charges see our free leaflet. Dia

Directory Enquiries 192
Tell the operator the town you require. Have

Emergency 999
Tell the operator what service you want.

Faults 151

Picture composition

1 *Look at these pictures. They show the everyday life of an unhealthy businessman. Under each picture write what he should do.* The first one is done for you.

He should eat less.
He shouldn't eat greasy food.

2 *Now answer these questions:*

a Do you think he does any exercise?
b Do you think he eats too much?
c What will happen if he continues like this?

3 *Now imagine that you are his doctor. You are writing him a letter. Write the middle two paragraphs. The first one should start:* You do not get enough exercise and you eat too much . . . *(Now describe his normal day.)*

The second one should start: For breakfast you should . . . *(Give him advice for dieting and exercise.)*

Discussion

1 *In groups, look at these pictures. Say what happens to you if you eat or drink too much or too little of each of them.*
The first one is done for you:

If you drink too much coffee, you'll get very nervous.

2 *Now decide how much of each item you should drink or eat each day:*

Two cups of coffee is probably enough each day.

3 *Now imagine you have to plan meals for a week. You can have three meals a day:* breakfast, a snack for lunch, dinner.

Plan the meals, making sure you get enough food!
Don't forget food like vegetables and fruit.
Don't forget drinks like milk and fruit juice.

Letter-writing

1 *Read the letter opposite from an Englishman to a foreign visitor.*

a Make a list of the things he should bring with him.
b Make a list of the things he need not bring with him.

2 *Imagine that an English friend of yours is going to visit you in your home town.* Besides visiting the town, you are also going on a skiing holiday (winter) or going on a trip along the coast/to the mountains (summer).

a Make a list of the things he/she should bring.
b Make a list of the things he/she doesn't need.

3 *Now writer a letter to your friend like the one on the next page.*
Tell him/her to bring the things from your first list:

Please bring . . .

Perhaps you should bring . . .

Tell him/her the things which he/she doesn't need:

You needn't bring . . .

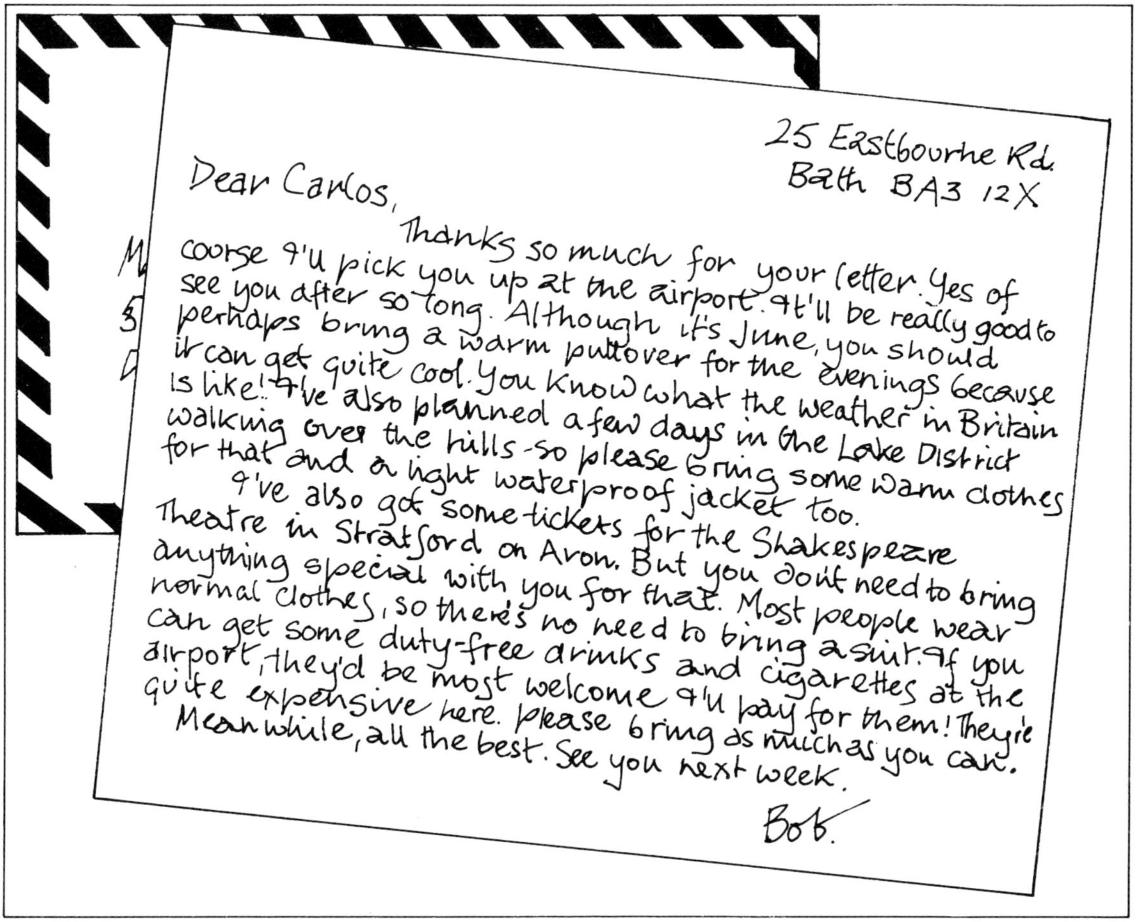

25 Eastbourne Rd.
Bath BA3 12X

Dear Carlos,

Thanks so much for your letter. Yes of course I'll pick you up at the airport. It'll be really good to see you after so long. Although it's June, you should perhaps bring a warm pullover for the evenings because it can get quite cool. You know what the weather in Britain is like! I've also planned a few days in the Lake District walking over the hills - so please bring some warm clothes for that and a light waterproof jacket too.

I've also got some tickets for the Shakespeare Theatre in Stratford on Avon. But you don't need to bring anything special with you for that. Most people wear normal clothes, so there's no need to bring a suit. If you can get some duty-free drinks and cigarettes at the airport, they'd be most welcome. I'll pay for them! They're quite expensive here. Please bring as much as you can.

Meanwhile, all the best. See you next week.

Bob.

Game

Look at this puzzle.

There are 25 words in it which are related to fitness and food.
They can be read from left to right, right to left, top to bottom, bottom to top or diagonally!

Try to find them.

F	V	P	O	A	Q	U	S	W	I	M	M	I	N	G
O	A	L	I	B	T	R	S	T	P	Z	I	L	N	N
O	M	T	O	D	I	L	E	O	T	Q	L	I	O	I
D	W	F	R	U	I	T	N	W	A	L	K	I	N	G
O	P	H	D	M	E	A	T	R	L	O	T	K	P	G
R	L	D	M	A	B	Y	I	O	M	S	B	D	H	O
Y	W	I	L	G	O	L	F	S	L	S	P	A	I	J
O	N	E	K	L	P	R	R	Q	K	C	R	O	O	P
G	A	T	R	W	B	U	A	C	D	I	F	M	R	L
H	T	L	S	E	D	N	G	Q	R	T	I	P	A	T
U	E	T	N	I	O	N	U	S	D	E	R	N	N	O
R	H	A	L	G	G	I	S	A	I	L	I	N	G	K
T	O	D	L	H	I	N	O	R	L	H	N	O	E	X
E	L	B	A	T	E	G	E	V	G	T	M	L	R	A
P	G	A	G	R	H	L	Q	X	L	A	I	T	O	S

(Key: jogging, swimming, smoking, milk, walking, fitness, slimming, diet, yoghurt, health, golf, weight, fruit, vegetable, running, skiing, athletics, orange, sailing, food, sport, meat, sugar, fat, tea.)

Unit Six

Reading: Leisure

Look at these figures. They show the leisure activities of men and women in Britain in 1977. The column on the left shows the different types of activity. The other two columns show the percentages of men and women who participate in them. Notice that many men and women participate in more than one leisure activity.

Open-air outings:	**Men**	**Women**
seaside	6	7
country	5	5
parks	3	4
Countryside activities	31	27
Entertainment, social and cultural activities:		
going to the cinema	11	10
visiting historic buildings	8	9
going to the theatre/ opera/ballet	4	6
going to museums/art galleries	4	3
amateur music/drama	4	3
attending leisure classes	1	3
going to fairs	2	2
going out for a meal/drink	71	57
dancing	14	16
social and voluntary work	8	9
Home-based activities:		
listening to records/tapes	64	60
gardening	49	35
games of skill	21	16
needlework/knitting	2	51
house repairs/DIY	51	22
hobbies	12	3
reading books	52	57

Answer these questions.

1 What do you think Countryside activities are?
2 What is the most popular social activity?
3 What is the second most popular social activity?
4 Which activities have a much larger number of women participating than men?
5 Do you think the results would be the same for your country? What differences might there be?

Getting around

1 *Listen to the conversation and write down the answers to the questions below.*

– What shall we do on Saturday night, Mary?
– I'd like to go out somewhere. What's on at the cinema?
– Oh, nothing really. I'd like to go to that concert.
– Oh. I'm not very keen on that. How about the theatre?
– OK, I think there's quite a good play on. Let me just check in the paper . . .

a Where does Mary want to go?
b Where does John want to go?
c Where do they decide to go?

2 *Practise the conversation with another student.*

3 *Practise the conversation using this information:*
Friday night/stay in/television/see that film/ a concert?/a good one.

4 *Listen to the conversation and write down the answers to the questions on page 39:*

– Well, I suppose we'd better decide about the holiday, then.
– Yes, Charles. I'd really like to go to Spain again. It was great fun there last year.
– Yes, but we can't afford it. I'd prefer to go camping and save some money.
– Can't we compromise somehow? Camping in England is no fun. It rains all the time.
– Yes, that's true. Well, we could go camping in France. Let's sit down and work out if we've got enough money . . .

a What does Charles want to do?
b What does Alison want to do?
c What do they finally decide to do?

5 *Practise the conversation with another student.*

6 *Practise the conversation using this information:*
Sweden/Portugal — save money/it's too hot/
France — not too expensive.

Listening

Listen to the tour guide's talk. Fill in the table and put the name under the pictures.

Day	City/Town	Leaving at	Things to be seen
Saturday			
Sunday			
Monday			

Telephoning

1 *Listen to this telephone conversation.*

– Eastbourne 66711.
– Could I speak to Bill, please?
– One moment, please.
– Bill Johnson.
– Hi, Bill. This is Peter Caversham. How are you?
– Fine thanks — and you?
– Fine. I was wondering what you and Mary are doing on Saturday night.
– Oh, I don't think we've got any plans yet.
– Well, we're having a small party. Would you both like to come?
– That sounds really nice. Let me check with Mary and call you back.
– Great. About 7.30?
– That sounds fine. Thanks a lot. I'll call you back this evening.
– Great. Bye.
– Bye.

2 *Practise the conversation with another student.*

3 *Practise the conversation with another student using this information:*
Friday night/dinner party/8.00.

4 *Practise the conversation with another student, inviting him/her to dinner/party/drink. Use your own information.*

Picture composition

Look at these pictures. They show various types of holiday and the sort of people who might take them.

1 *Write one or two sentences about each picture saying why you think that those people take that type of holiday.*

2 *Now choose one of the pictures and say why you think the people have chosen that type of holiday. Write a paragraph about the people and what they might do on their holiday.*

3 *Now write a paragraph about the type of holiday that you enjoy. Give reasons and also say what you expect to do on holiday.*

Discussion

1 *Look at this table and fill in the first column about yourself:*

Leisure activity	For yourself Hrs per week	For your group Average hrs per week
TV		
Reading		
Sports (which ones?)		
Meeting friends		
Going out for meal/drink		
Other (what?)		

2 *Get together in groups and compare your answers. Fill in the second column for your group. Specify the most popular types of sports and other activities.*

3 *Answer these questions:*

a How does your group differ from the chart on p38?

b Does your group watch more or less TV than the people interviewed for the chart?

c Does your group do more sports than the people interviewed for the chart?

Letter-writing

1 *Look at this invitation to a party:*

We're having a party!!

on: Saturday 15th

at: 9.00 pm

in: John's flat

(15, Albermarle Rd)

Bring a bottle and a friend!!

Write a similar invitation to a friend for a dinner party.

Use an address you know.

2 *Look at this letter:*

22, Whitehorse Park
Reading RD4 2RT

14th June.

Dear Jane,

John and I are going up to the Lake District next weekend (19th–21st). Would you like to join us? We're staying at a friend's cottage while he's away. There's plenty of room.

We're travelling up by car on Friday evening and then back again Sunday evening. We're planning to do some hill-walking on Saturday and Sunday if the weather is good enough. In the evenings we're going to visit some of the local pubs.

It would be really nice if you could come as well. I'll telephone you on Tuesday night to see if you want to come.

Much love

Cath

Write a similar letter to a friend about a weekend you're planning.

Use this information:
friend's flat in London/Friday – Sunday/ cinema and clubs/train.

Game

Look at these pictures. Under each picture there are some words.
Make up a story related to the picture using the words underneath.
You must use all *the words.*

car, next year, mountains, tent, expensive

disco, Saturday, not enough money, Mike?, TV

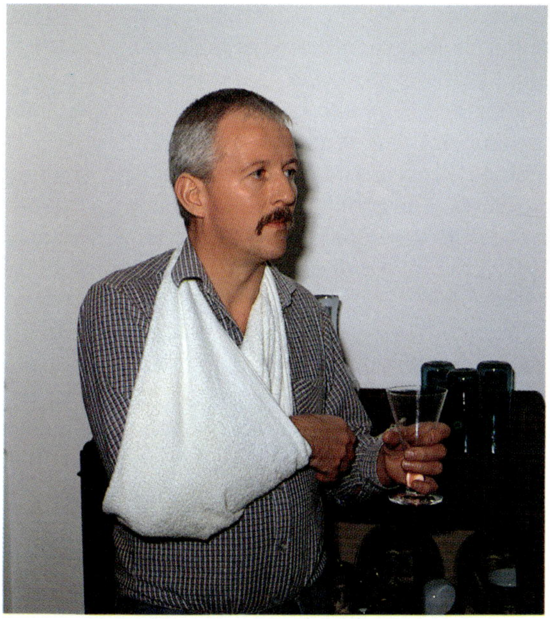

beach, shell, newspaper, coat, cigarettes

doctor, diet, wife, Olympics, hospital

Unit Seven

Reading: Computers and things!

Answer these questions.

1 Write down the names of the different parts of a home computer.

2 When you buy a computer program, you need to make sure of two things. The first is whether you need a cassette or disk. What is the other important thing?

3 Why is a disk drive better than a cassette recorder?

4 What do you need if you want to use your computer for word-processing?

Computers are used in schools, in offices and in homes. They are becoming smaller, cheaper and available to a wider range of people.

A basic home computer system includes a computer keyboard, a display screen and a cassette recorder. That is all you need to get started. You buy computer programs (software) on cassettes. These programs must be in the same computer language as your computer (there are several different 'languages').

You can play games, keep records, do arithmetic and begin to write your own programs. The problem is that it is slow to transfer the program from the cassette recorder to the computer. To speed things up, it is possible to buy a disk drive and use disks instead of cassettes to store programs. It then takes only a few seconds to load the program. You can write a program then save it by transferring it back onto the disk. The program is then ready to load and use again when you need it.

Another 'extra' to improve the system is a printer, which makes it possible to use the computer for word-processing. For example, you might want to type in a letter, alter it, and then print out the final version.

How much you pay depends on which computer and which extras you buy. One important thing to consider is the size of the memory. A larger memory (48K instead of 16K) will allow you to run and write more complicated programs.

Getting around

1 *Listen to this conversation:*

– Good morning, sir.
– Good morning. I'm looking for a new jacket. Something fairly casual that I can wear all the time.
– Well, sir, we have this at £35, or this better-quality one at £55.
– Oh dear, I didn't want to spend as much as £55.
– Of course, sir. But it will last longer.
– Yes. Um, I'd better think about it for a day or two. Thank you very much.
– Not at all, sir. Goodbye.

2 *Practise the conversation with another student.*

3 *Practise the conversation with another student using this information:*

suit/£99/£159; blouse/£15/£25; shoes/£30/£50

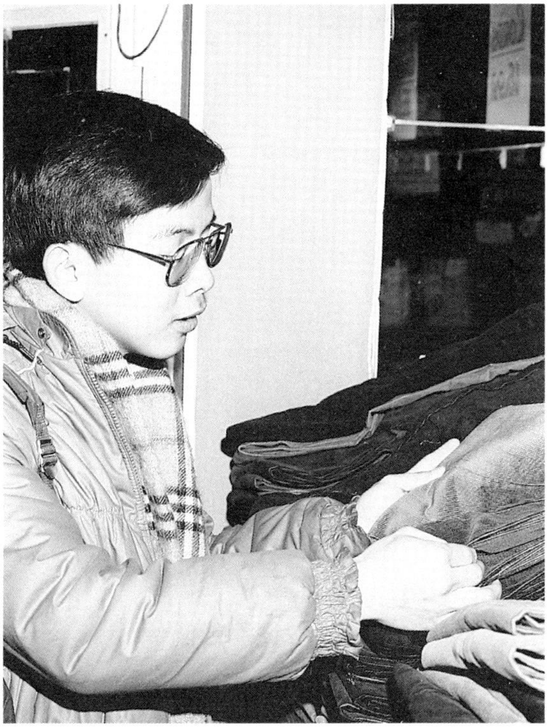

Listening

1 Mrs Black has had an interview for a job. She's a bit worried about certain things. She asks the interviewer some questions. *Fill in this table with the answers.*

	Word-processor	Computer
Description		
Use		
Length of training		

2 *Listen to the first part of the conversation and answer:*

a What is Jane's best subject?
b Is she getting better in all subjects?
c What is her worst subject?
d What's happening to her marks here?

3 *Listen to the second part of the conversation and answer.*

a What could her father use the computer for?
b When is Jane going to work out a program for her father?

4 *Listen to the whole conversation again and answer:*

a Does Jane like computing?
b Does she spend a lot of time with the computer?
c Does her father know how to use the computer?
d Do you think Jane will make a profit from computing?

Telephoning

1 *Listen to the first conversation and write down what you have to do to telephone Milan.*

– Operator. Can I help you?
– Um yes, could you give me the international operator, please?
– For which country, sir?
– Italy.
– Please dial 155, sir.
– Thanks.
– International operator. Which country do you want?
– Italy, please.
– Which city, sir?
– Milan.
– You can dial the number direct, sir.
– Oh, can I? What's the code please?
– 01039 and then 2 for Milan.
– 01039 and then 2 for Milan. Thank you very much.
– And it's cheaper after 8 o'clock in the evening.
– Right, thanks a lot. Bye.
– Bye.

2 *Practise the conversation with another student.*

3 *Practise the conversation with another student using this information:*

France/Lyon/01033/7
Germany/Dortmund/01040/231
Spain/Valencia/01034/6

4 *Listen to the second conversation and write down the name and address and telephone number required.*

– Operator. Can I help you?
– I want to find a number in Austria. Can you help me?
– Would you dial 153 please, madam.
– Oh, OK, thanks.
– International directory. Which country, please?
– Austria, please.
– And the city or area, madam?
– Salzburg.
– And the name, please?
– Hofmeister.
– Could you spell that, please?
– H-O-F-M-E-I-S-T-E-R.
– Thank you. And the initials?
– J, R.
– Thank you, madam. One moment, please.
– OK.
– Is the address Hofgarten 16?
– Yes.
– The number is Salzburg 177438. Do you know the code?
– Yes, thank you very much. Goodbye.
– Bye.

5 *Practise the conversation with another student.*

6 *Practise the conversation with another student using your own information.*

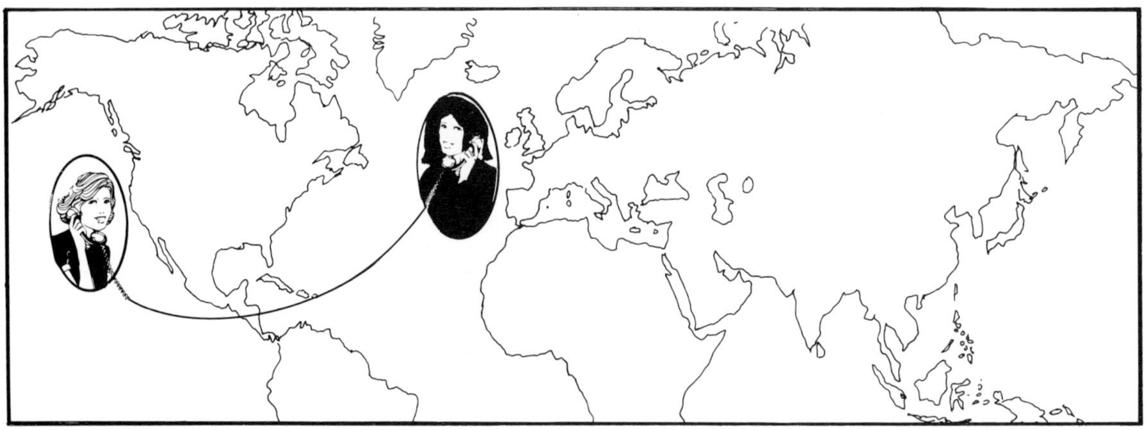

Picture composition

1 *Look at these pictures of offices. Write down under each picture some of the things you can see.*

2 *Write a paragraph saying which office you think is the more efficient. Give reasons.*

3 *Write another paragraph saying which office you think is more friendly. Give reasons.*

4 *Write a third paragraph saying which office you would prefer to work in. Give reasons.*

Discussion

1 *Find out who in the group has used a computer.*

2 *Have you seen a computer used when booking:*

a a theatre ticket?
b a train journey?
c a flight?
d a holiday?

Did it make things easier and quicker?

3 *Would you like to own a home computer? What would you use it for?*

4 *Who should be allowed to keep information about you on a computer?*

a the police?
b your doctor?
c the government?
d your bank?
e the company you work for?

Should they be able to exchange information about you?

5 *Computers can work much more quickly than people. Can you think of any advantages and disadvantages of computers being used more?*

Letter-writing

1 *Read this advertisement.*

> **Flights! Flights! Flights!**
>
> We can offer you flights to most places.
>
> Here are some examples:
>
> Athens £150; New York £120; Cairo £210; Rome £125.
>
> Write to us for more details at:
>
> **Memphis Travel**
> 6 Charles St., London SW3B 2TQ

2 *Now read the letter opposite on page 49.*

3 *Read this advertisement.*

> **Accommodation!**
>
> We can offer cheap accommodation in many holiday resorts.
>
> Here are some examples:
>
> Tenerife £20 per night; Athens £15 per night; Rome £25 per night; New York £35 per night.
>
> Write to us for more details at:
>
> **Sunbird Travel,**
> 23 Grafley Place, London NW3 4TH

4 *Write a letter to the travel company.*
Ask about cheaper accommodation in Athens and Rome.
Say that you are a student.
Say that you are travelling in June.

26 Charleston Road
Overton
Reading RG3 4RY

28 April 1985

Memphis Travel
6 Charles Street
London SW3B 2TQ

Dear Sir

I am writing to ask for some flight details. I am particularly interested in your flights to Athens and Rome.

First of all, do you have any cheaper flights than those advertised? I am interested in anything under £125 for Athens and £100 for Rome.

Secondly, I am a full-time student: does this mean I can get cheaper flights or a discount?

Thirdly, I would like to travel in September. Are flights cheaper then than in the summer?

I hope to hear from you soon.

Yours faithfully

David Stone

David Stone

Game

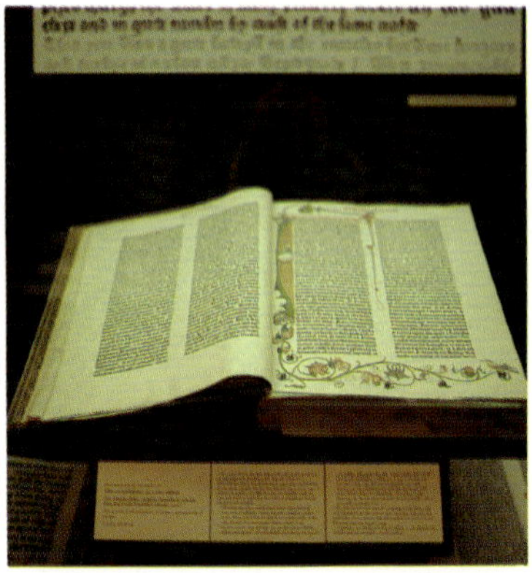

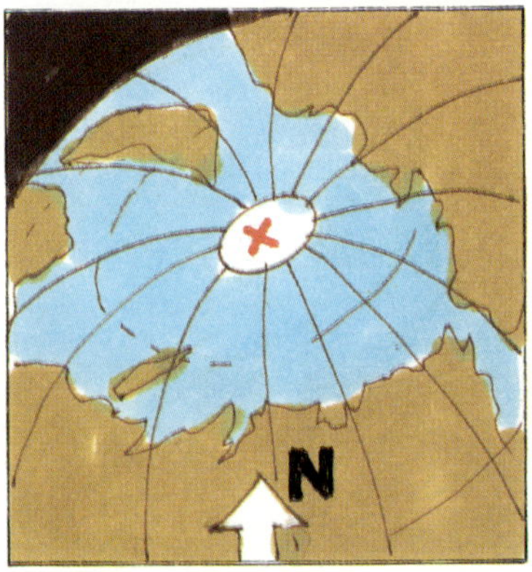

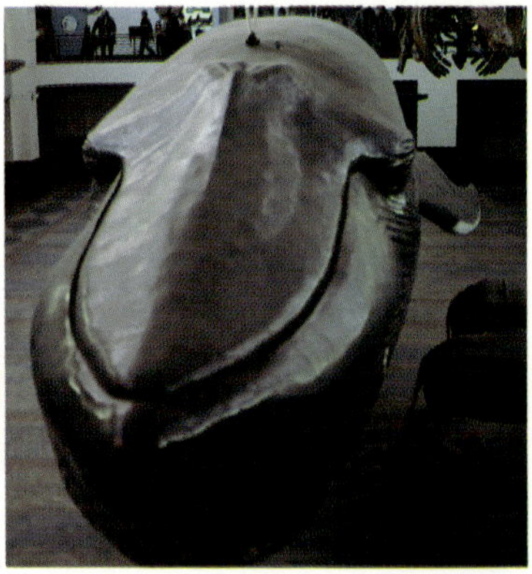

Quiz

Look at these pictures. Each of them shows an object which is the biggest/oldest/widest/etc. *Say what each of them is and also try to name them.*

For example: The Nile is the longest river in the world.

Class survey

Ask the other students and complete this survey:

1 Who is the oldest in the class?
2 Who is the youngest in the class?
3 Who lives nearest the school?
4 Who lives furthest from the school?
5 Who spent the most money yesterday?
6 Who ate the most yesterday?

Unit Eight

Answer these questions:

1 Why do people love Volkswagen Beetles?
2 Why do people love Levi's jeans?
3 How old is the design of the jeans?
4 What is a cult object?
5 Give two more examples of cult objects.
6 What is important about cult objects?
7 Match the pictures with each of the items mentioned.

Reading: Design and style

Why do people love a Volkswagen Beetle or a Citroen 2CV? They can be inefficient and noisy. They're old. But, for many people, they have character and charm. If there is a natural shape for a small car, then this is it. We can say the same about Levi's jeans. They are the basic shape for casual trousers. They are strong and well-made. The design hasn't changed for over a hundred years.

Both the cars and the jeans have become 'cult objects'. Cult objects are the 'stars' of modern design and technology. They may be expensive, they may be cheap. A Rolex watch may cost £700. A box of Swan Vesta matches costs a few pence. The price is not important. It is the timeless quality of the 'right design' which is important.

Getting around

1 *Listen to the conversation.*

– What's that car?
– It's a Lamborghini, I think.
– Isn't it fantastic!
– Yes, but expensive!

2 *Practise the conversation with another student.*

3 *Practise the conversation with another student using this information:*
car/Rolls-Royce/beautiful;
stereo/Bang & Olufsen/superb;
television/Sinclair/tiny.

4 *Listen to the conversation.*

– That's a beautiful pullover.
– Yes, it is. Shall we go in and see how much it is?
– OK. But I haven't got much money on me.
– Nor have I. But let's ask.

5 *Practise the conversation with another student.*

6 *Practise the conversation with another student using this information:*

good-looking suit/much money; interesting book/any money; great video/enough money.

Listening

Look at the people in the photographs on the next page.
Listen to the comments on their clothes.
Discuss these comments with others in the class.

Telephoning

– Turner Travel Agency, good morning.
– Good morning. I'd like to ask about travelling to Edinburgh, please.
– Yes, sir. I'll put you through. One moment, please.
– Good morning. Can I help you?
– Yes, I'd like to ask about travelling to Edinburgh, please.
– Certainly, sir. By train or coach or plane?
– By train or coach, please.
– One moment, please, sir . . . Well, the coach is the cheapest but it takes the longest. The easiest way by coach is to travel overnight. It takes about eight hours and costs £23 return.
– That's fine, but I see what you mean about the time.
– Well, by train it's quicker but more expensive. There are various cheap fares starting at about £30 return, but you are restricted in your travel times. The journey takes . . . um . . . about four and a half hours on average.
– OK. That gives me some idea. I'll call back tomorrow. Thank you.
– Thank you, sir. Goodbye.
– Goodbye.

1 *Listen to the conversation and fill in this table:*

	Price	Journey time
Coach		
Train		

2 *Practise the conversation with another student.*

3 *Practise the conversation with another student using this information:*

To	By	Journey time	Price
Manchester	coach	3½ hrs	£18
	train	2 hrs 40 mins	£24
Newcastle	coach	5½ hrs	£21
	train	3½ hrs	£27

Picture composition

Look at these pictures of various fashions and clothes.

1 *Write underneath each picture the type of clothes worn. Choose from this list:*

dinner jacket — casual wear — business suit — evening dress

2 *Write underneath each picture who might wear these clothes and on what occasions.*

3 *Choose three of the pictures and write a paragraph about the clothes and the people who might wear them.*

4 *Write a paragraph about the clothes you like to wear and on what occasions. Write a few sentences about clothes you don't like wearing and why.*

Discussion

1 *Look at these two pictures. One of them shows a basic object; the other shows an object with unnecessary features:*

This lamp is a basic lamp. It has an arm to change its position. It has a basic bulb and shade.

This lamp has many unnecessary things. Look at the shade: it has a frilly edge. Look at the base: it has a complex design on it.

2 *Now look at these pairs of pictures. What are the unnecessary features of the objects in the pictures on the right?*

3 *Now look at these pictures. What are the features which are necessary in each object and what are unnecessary?*

4 *Now discuss in groups:*

a Why do you think all the unnecessary features were put on/in the objects?

b How many of them are modern and how many are older?

Letter-writing

1 *Read this 'Thank you' note.*

2 *Write a 'Thank you' note to a friend.*

Say thank you for a dinner party.

Mention the people you met.

Compliment him/her on the food.

Dear John, Monday 16th

Just a quick note to say thank you for the great party on Saturday night. It was really nice to meet so many interesting people. And thanks for the wonderful food! See you soon.

Love Bill

3 *Read this 'Thank you' letter.*

4 *Now write a letter to some people you have stayed with in a foreign country.*

Thank them for your stay.

Apologise for any difficulties you may have caused.

Describe your return journey.

State your immediate plans.

Invite them to stay with you.

Thank them again.

Rosengarten 23
5000, Koeln 3

Sept 27th

Dear Mr and Mrs Cardew,

Thank you so much for letting me stay with you for the last three weeks. You gave me a wonderful introduction to England and to English people. I hope that I didn't make too much trouble for you, especially with the food!

I arrived home safely last night and slept for 12 hours after the long journey. It's nice to be back, but now I have to start preparing for school again.

If you would like to come to Germany, please write and tell me. My parents would love to meet you.

Thank you again for everything you did for me.

With my very best wishes,

Carl Jung

Game

Quiz on Britain

See how quickly you can answer these questions about Britain.

1 What are the names of these places?

2

- **a** What is BR?
- **b** What are the names of the TV channels in Britain which have advertising?
- **c** What are the names of the two Houses of Parliament?
- **d** What is the Tube?
- **e** What is the capital of Wales?
- **f** Where is the Lake District?
- **g** Where is the highest mountain in Britain?
- **h** Name two games which are played in Britain in the summer.

Tapescript and Notes

Unit One

Listening 1–3

Hello, everybody. My name's Rick Hudson and I'd like to welcome you all to the school. I hope you've all had a good night's rest after your long journey. I'm going to tell you some of the things that you'll be doing while you are staying here.

First of all, you probably want to know where the classrooms are in the school and what they are used for. Please look at the plan you've been given. It shows the ground floor of the school. You can see the main entrance on the right. That's the entrance from the car park. As you come in from the car park, you'll find my office on your left. It's easy to recognise — it has my name on the door. Next to my room, also on the left, are the toilets — ladies and gentlemen's. Beyond them, also on the left, is my secretary's office. So those are the first four doors on the left.

Now, opposite these rooms is classroom 1. So, when you come in through the main entrance from the car park, classroom 1 is the first room on the right. Groupwork classes take place in here. The teacher's table is in the centre of the room and the desks and chairs are arranged in groups of five. There are twenty students' desks and chairs.

Next to classroom 1 is classroom 2. This is the second room on the right as you come in through the main entrance. Discussion classes take place in here. The chairs and tables are arranged in a square. This means that you can all see one another during a discussion. Oh — I nearly forgot the most important rooms — the kitchen and snackbar. These are next to my secretary's office opposite the entrance to classroom 2.

And next to the snack bar is classroom 3. It's smaller than the other classrooms. The seats are arranged in rows and it's equipped as a language laboratory. All your language laboratory classes take place in classroom 3. You may have other classes in there too.

The biggest room is classroom 4. You won't normally have classes in here. It's used as a film room or lecture hall or as a party room in the evenings. Sometimes two or three classes may be in classroom 4 for a talk. Now, upstairs on the first floor . . .

Listening 4–6

– Silvia, I'm sorry I won't be able to come shopping with you this morning. I've got to help Mrs Smith next door.

– Oh, it doesn't really matter. But would you mind very much telling me where to buy things? I'm still not very sure about English shops.

– Yes, of course. Umm, have you got the shopping list?

– Yes, but it's not written down!

– OK, so, um, here's a map. Well, get off the bus at the corner of High Street and Portsmouth Street. The bus stops immediately after the junction outside Smith's the jewellers on the High Street.

– Bus stop outside Smith's the jewellers on the High Street. OK. Well, I need some pens and paper and things like that for school on Monday. What do you call all those things?

– Oh, stationery. The best place for that is Ryman's. It's right next door to Smith's on the High Street. Just walk up the High Street a few yards and it's there on the corner of George Street.

– Ryman's, corner of High Street and George Street. And I want to look for a good cheap pullover.

– What about Marks and Spencer's? They're reasonable. That's the big shop on the High Street just before Portsmouth Street. Walk back down the High Street, past Portsmouth Street and there it is.

– Marks and Spencer's, High Street before Portsmouth Street. OK. And some film for the camera?

– The best place is probably Dixon's on Portsmouth Street. Well, Smith's is on the corner of Portsmouth Street and the High Street. Um, go round into Portsmouth Street; after Smith's, there's a café and then Dixon's, so it's the second shop down Portsmouth Street after Smith's. The café has got good cakes too — you should try them!

– Um, yes. Well, I've also got to get some wine for the party tonight.

– Cheap but good, eh? Sainsbury's is probably the best. They're further away on Canford Street between College Road and Clement Street. Can you see that big block on Canford Street between College Road and Clement Street? That's Sainsbury's. While you're in there, could you do me a favour?

– Yes, of course.

– I'd like a pound of cheddar cheese. And theirs is particularly good.

– OK. So, wine and a pound of cheddar cheese from Sainsbury's on Canford Street. Well, that's about it, I think. Maybe I will go to that café. The cakes sound really good.

– Oh, and the bus stop for the bus coming home is on the High Street opposite Marks and Spencer's. Number 37 bus, OK?

– Right. Thanks.

Discussion 1

– . . . And now I'd like to welcome Cheryl Baker from the Committee for International Understanding. Cheryl, can I ask you about voluntary service abroad? What does it involve?
– Well, first of all, I should perhaps mention two of the main organisations involved — Voluntary Service Overseas (that's VSO) and International Voluntary Service (that's IVS). I'll give the addresses at the end of the programme.
– Great, thanks. Tell me, Cheryl, what age of people are they looking for?
– Well, the usual age range is somewhere between 21 and 55. Someone who's younger than 21 may not have the skills or experience needed. And someone over 55 might find it hard to live in a different or difficult climate. But there are exceptions to the general rule.
– Um, I see. You mentioned skills and experience. Are these necessary for the volunteer?
– Yes, normally. A person who wants to go abroad as a volunteer should have some skills to offer and at least some experience in a trade or a profession. This trade or profession will be of use to the country which the person is sent to. You'd be surprised how many different types of work there are. All sorts of people become volunteers.
– Could you give us some examples?
– Well, there are many obvious ones such as doctors, nurses and teachers. But there are also accountants, garage mechanics, secretaries. In fact, almost any profession you can think of.
– And how long do they normally stay abroad?
– Usually it's two years. I think that most people find that they spend some part of the first year getting used to the food, the climate and the job. So one year would probably be too short. It would also be difficult for someone to commit themselves to staying in a totally strange place for more than two years. Perhaps they may want to renew their contract after two years.
– And what about money, Cheryl?
– They are paid enough to live on, so it varies from country to country. Enough to live on means that they have enough for food, drink and basic clothing. Accommodation is usually provided. If it isn't, then they get a higher salary.

Discussion 2

– Why do people go on voluntary service when they probably could be earning more money at home?
– There are many different reasons. I think that one thing that all volunteers share is a wish to help others. On a personal level, people go for many reasons: some want to experience a different way of life in another culture. They do indeed live very differently from their life at home. Others may be unemployed or even retired. They feel that they are doing something useful. Others may already have worked abroad and have enjoyed the experience, so they want to continue working abroad. And there are many, many other reasons.
– Yes, I can see that. Well, thank you Cheryl. Now what about those addresses . . .

Section 1	Reading: The National Trust Description of the National Trust.
Section 2	Getting around Describing the weather.
Section 3	Listening Descriptions of a school layout and a town centre.
Section 4	Telephoning Getting to speak to the right person.
Section 5	Picture composition Describing old and new buildings.
Section 6	Discussion Description of Voluntary Service and discussion of its usefulness.
Section 7	Letter-writing Describing arrival in a new town, and the town.
Section 8	Game Describing the differences between two pictures.

Unit Two

Listening 1

When I arrived from Jamaica, I was only fifteen. That was in 1968. My parents sent for me. They had been living here for ten years and they wanted me to go to school here. So I came. I remember the day I left Jamaica — it was beautifully sunny and warm in October '68 — London was rainy and cold and I didn't want to be here. Still, I came. Originally, we lived in London, but then I moved out when I went to college and now I've got a job as a computer programmer with a company in Bristol. I like living in Bristol, it's not too big. But I still miss Jamaica. The people there are much more open and friendly, and of course the climate is not cold and damp like England. But the job in Bristol is good — it pays well and it's interesting work. I don't have too many problems being black. At work, people respect me and, socially, things are OK.

Listening 2

My parents came here in 1957 and I was born here three years later in 1960. They came here to earn more money — my father knew he could work in a British factory. They lived in Pakistan and were quite poor.

I've been back to Pakistan and I don't really like it there — I feel more British than Pakistani. Anyway, my father got a job immediately in 1957 in a factory in London, and my mother stayed at home with the children. My father had to work very hard because they had four children. I'm the youngest. After my 'A' levels, I studied engineering and I'm now an engineer with a company in London. I live in east London and I've got a couple of kids. To me, there are several advantages to living in England: a good job, more money than I could have in Pakistan and plenty of friends. I suppose there are some disadvantages: people at work think I'm taking a job away from a British person (but I've got a British passport and was born here) and most of my friends are Pakistani too. I feel I'm British, but I'm not really accepted by the British.

Section 1	Reading: Minorities in Britain History of recent immigration to Britain.
Section 2	Getting around Hiring a bicycle/tent/boat.
Section 3	Listening Immigrants talk about how/why they came to Britain.
Section 4	Telephoning Leaving a message.
Section 5	Picture Composition People in a foreign setting.
Section 6	Discussion Two foreigners explain why they live in Britain. Discussion of living in foreign countries.
Section 7	Letter-writing Complaining about bicycle hire.
Section 8	Game Guessing a person's job.

Unit Three

Listening 1

– And what about you, John? Any thoughts on next year?
– Not really, sir. It looks like unemployment, though. I'm getting rather depressed about it.
– Well, don't give up on other things yet. It might be better for you to stay on at school, you know. I know the job market is very difficult at the moment. If you stay on at school, you could work for some extra qualifications which may help you later. You know, when the job market is very difficult, it's always useful to have those few extra qualifications. You could always repeat subjects where you've got a low grade. Or you might find that some other subjects interest you.
– Couldn't I go to a further education college?
– Umm. That's also a possibility. The range of subjects there is much wider than at school. You might find more things there to interest you. On the other hand it's a completely new start — you know, getting to know teachers and their methods, making new friends and so on. It could be better or it could be worse! It depends very much on how you feel.
– Yeah, I see what you mean. OK, and what are these Youth Training Schemes everyone's talking about?
– Well, they're training courses which are very practical. They're run by the Government and you can find them in many different places. They also cover many different types of training. You even get paid something while you're doing them.
– But it doesn't guarantee me a job, right?
– No, that's true, but it may help.
– OK. So, school, further education college and Youth Training Scheme. Hmm. Can I see some more details?
– Yes, of course. Here are some leaflets. Why don't you look at them and come back when you've thought about it?

Listening 2

– Dad? Can I talk to you?
– Sure, John. Is it about university?
– How did you guess?
– I thought the question would come up fairly soon!
– Oh. I don't quite know where to start.
– Well, what choices do you have?
– Umm. I can go to university or I can go on a sandwich course.
– Well, let's go through each one.
– OK. University. The problem here is money. I know I may get a grant, but it isn't very much and I don't want you giving me money all the time. I wouldn't feel very independent, you know.
– But it means you'd probably get a better job at the end.
– Well . . . probably, but that's not really guaranteed. And I'd like to feel that I'm earning something now.
– OK. What about the sandwich course?
– Umm. This is a sort of a combination of job and study. A company employs you, but lets you study for one or two days a week and usually pays the fees. So you're getting training which is directly related to the job you're doing. It's good, this. You get the qualifications and the experience and you get paid.
– A full salary?
– No, but you go on to full salary when you've finished training.

Section 1	Reading: Secondary school education 'O' and 'A' level exams.
Section 2	Getting around Getting something cleaned/asking about repairs.
Section 3	Listening Talking about leaving school.

Section 4 Telephoning
Arranging to meet someone.

Section 5 Picture composition
Getting a better job through evening classes.

Section 6 Discussion
Deciding who has the best qualifications for a job.

Section 7 Letter-writing
Inviting someone.

Section 8 Game
Guessing what is in the picture.

Unit Four

Listening

Speaker 1

I like watching TV. I can relax in the evenings after work. I don't have to think at all. It's nice to sit there with a beer and be entertained. But I don't like all the programmes.

What I really like watching is sport. On Saturday afternoon you can't get me away from the telly. I have it on all afternoon. I don't think there's enough sport on TV. There should be one channel which you can switch on at any time — all sport. A lot of people feel like me. They want to be entertained and to relax. I'd like to see a lot more sport like rugby and cricket.

There are too many news programmes. They don't tell you anything. Sure, I like to see the headlines, but I can also read those in a newspaper. I usually look at the headlines on the six o'clock news, but that's enough for me. And things like Panorama or other documentaries — they're so boring. A good rugby match is much more interesting.

There's also too much entertainment for kids. There's a couple of hours in the afternoon and even some in the mornings. They shouldn't be watching telly anyway. They should be getting on with their homework. I don't like to see kids sitting in front of the telly just staring at it. They should get out and play with their friends or do their homework or whatever they have to do.

Let's have more sport, I say!

Speaker 2

I like watching TV sometimes. It depends very much on the programmes which are on. I can't sit back and be entertained. I have to get involved, or else it has to be really interesting. I think there are too many soap operas and stupid series. I know a lot of people watch them, but I can't. They're so boring. They're . . . well, they don't tell you anything. They don't inform you or give you anything new.

There aren't enough news programmes. I don't mean the six o'clock news or the nine o'clock news. They're fine. We need more discussion programmes about things that are happening. And documentaries. All sorts of documentaries are really interesting. Animal programmes, how other people live and so on. They're fascinating and give you so much knowledge of the world.

There's really too much entertainment on television, you know. The programmes are there so that you can sit back and you don't have to think. There should be more programmes which make you think a bit or which educate you. Or give you some useful information.

Section 1 Reading: Television
Television programmes.

Section 2 Getting around
Asking about excursions.

Section 3 Listening
Opinions about what's on television.

Section 4 Telephoning
Asking for travel information.

Section 5 Picture composition
Opinions of TV programmes.

Section 6 Discussion
Choosing from news items for a news programme.

Section 7 Letter-writing
Changing a date/appointment.

Section 8 Game
Anagrams.

Unit Five

Listening 1

– Good morning, Dr Jones.
– Good morning, Mr Harrison. What can I do for you?
– Well, advice, actually. I'm thinking of taking up some sport, perhaps jogging, because I feel unfit. Is there anything I should do medically? Do you want to give me a check-up?
– Well, you've got no record of heart trouble, but I'll give you a quick check-up . . . That all seems fine.
– Is there anything I should or shouldn't do, Dr Jones?
– Yes. You should start jogging very slowly. Just walk fast at first if necessary. I've seen one programme that says you should jog for five minutes then walk for five minutes, then jog for five minutes and so on. That seems to me to be very sensible at first.
– That is about all I could manage at the moment.
– But you should do it regularly, say three times a week. If you do it one day, and then forget it for a week or so, that won't do you any good. It's got to be regular.
– Self-discipline, huh?
– Yes, I'm afraid so. And you should try and follow a

sensible diet. I mean you shouldn't eat more just because you're jogging. I think you'll find that your appetite will go down a bit with jogging anyway.
– Good. Anything else?
– Yes, perhaps you should look at an exercise programme which you can use with your jogging. Because jogging only exercises the lower half of your body. How about something for the upper half, too?
– Hmm, good idea. So: start slowly, take regular exercise, care with diet and perhaps an exercise programme. Well, thank you very much doctor, that's been a great help.
– Not at all. If you have any problems, come back and let's talk about it.
– Right. Goodbye.
– Goodbye.

Listening 2

– John, we've got to go on a diet!
– Oh no, not again. It never works for me.
– It would work if you listened to me and made an effort.
– All right, what is it this time?
– Well, first of all, we should plan a balanced diet. We should make sure that we're eating all the necessary vitamins and minerals and things like that.
– That sounds like homework!
– Don't worry. I've got a list of all the things here and loads of recipes for all sorts of meals. Secondly, we shouldn't try to lose weight quickly. It doesn't work, because you lose energy and feel hungry all the time. I think it's better to feel good and lose weight slowly.
– So how long is this diet going to go on?
– Until we feel we're the right weight! Maybe each of us should give up something which is bad for us. You know — I should give up cakes and you should give up sugar in tea and coffee.
– Ugh!
– Oh, come on, you can do it! It'll make life cheaper as well.
– True. Cakes are getting quite expensive!
– And how about some exercise? We should take up swimming again. We both enjoyed that, didn't we?
– Yes. I would like to go swimming again. All right, let me think about it for a day or two.
– Why think about it? Why not start now?
– Because I'm hungry.

Section 1 Reading: Fitness and diet
Giving up sugar.

Section 2 Getting around
Deciding on food.

Section 3 Listening
Advice on jogging/diet.

Section 4 Telephoning
Getting information from Directory Enquiries.

Section 5 Picture composition
Giving advice on diet/exercise.

Section 6 Discussion
Recommending a good diet.

Section 7 Letter-writing
Advising someone about what to take on a trip.

Section 8 Game
Word square.

Unit Six

Listening

Good evening, everybody. My name's Mike Charlton and I'm your guide during your stay in London. I'd like to welcome you to London and tell you about the trips we'll be making while you're here.

It starts fairly easily tomorrow in London. First of all, we're going to see St Paul's Cathedral in the morning and then in the afternoon there's a tour of famous buildings in London. On Sunday there's a coach tour to Oxford and Stratford-on-Avon. In Oxford, we're going to look round the beautiful old buildings of the University. In Stratford-on-Avon we're going to visit Shakespeare's house and the Royal Shakespeare Company Theatre.

On Monday, I'm afraid we have to start quite early — at 8 o'clock! The coach is going to take us to Bath, which is about a hundred miles west of London. It's a very beautiful city which was built in the eighteenth century. It's also got some very fine Roman ruins including the Roman Baths — probably the best example of Roman architecture in northern Europe.

Well, ladies and gentlemen, that's our programme. London tomorrow, Oxford and Stratford on Sunday and Bath on Monday. If you'd like some more details or have any questions, please don't hesitate to ask. Yes, madam? . . .

Section 1 Reading: Leisure
Table and text on leisure activities.

Section 2 Getting around
Planning a night out/holiday.

Section 3 Listening
Introduction to a tour by a tour guide.

Section 4 Telephoning
Inviting someone.

Section 5 Picture composition
Holidays for different types of people.

Section 6 Discussion
Leisure activities.

Section 7 Letter-writing
Invitation to a party/weekend away.

Section 8 Game
Making up stories based on pictures.

Unit Seven

Listening 1

– Well, now, Mrs Black, do you have any questions about the job?
– Yes, I do, really. I'm a bit worried about this word-processing.
– There really is no need to worry about it. Your application form says that you can type quite fast. We'll give you training in the word-processor. It's really just an advanced typewriter. And it has a memory so that you don't have to type a regular letter again and again. You'll get used to it. The training only takes about a month. And you'll find that it's easier to check and correct mistakes than on a normal typewriter.
– Oh, that sounds fine. Erm, what is this computer? I'm not sure about that either.
– Well, we give you training in that as well. But that comes later — after you've worked with the word processor. Again, it's very much like a typewriter. You'll be using it to get information from its memory. Really, it's just like a large filing cabinet, except that there's no paper involved. You type out the reference numbers or the subject and the information appears on a television screen.
– Oh, that doesn't sound too difficult. How long would the training for that take?
– Probably a couple of months. We hope you can do that part-time during your working hours.
– Hm. That sounds fine. So the first bit of training would be with the word processor for about a month and then a two-month part-time period with the computer?
– Yes, that's about right. Exact details can be worked out later, of course.
– OK. Oh yes, about pay . . .

Listening 2–4

– Dad, Dad!
– Coming! . . . What is it?
– Look at this program I've just put in. It shows all my marks at school. And I'm getting better in most subjects.
– What's that one?
– French. That's the worst one.
– Yes, I can see that. You're getting lower marks than you used to. Why?
– Because I'm not interested in it, I suppose. But look at this — my maths marks are really good.
– Yes, probably because you spend so much time with the computer.
– But, look, my maths marks are the highest in the class.
– Umm, OK, but I still worry about your French.
– Why don't you have a go with the computer, Dad? It's easier than you think.
– Well, maybe, but not now.
– You could use it for your accounting for the shop, you know.
– Umm, I suppose I could.
– Do you want me to work out a program for it?
– Maybe. But *after* the end of term.
– Oh, OK. I understand.
– I might even pay you something for it.
– Erm, Dad? Does that mean we're in business together?

Section 1 Reading: Computers and things!
Starting a home computer system.

Section 2 Getting around
Comparing clothes/cameras.

Section 3 Listening
Attitudes to computers.

Section 4 Telephoning
Getting information from International Directory Enquiries.

Section 5 Picture composition
Comparing two working environments.

Section 6 Discussion
Uses of a computer.

Section 7 Letter-writing
Replying to travel advertisements.

Section 8 Game
Superlatives.

Unit Eight

Listening 1

I think she looks awful with all that orange hair. And it's such a strange shape. Why does she have to make her hair orange? And what has she got through her nose? A pin? And it's got something on it — a jewel or something bright, anyway. I can understand earrings, but I can't understand people who wear pins in their noses. Her leather skirt looks pretty awful too. And it's much too short. Especially in this weather. It looks really silly going around in a short skirt in cold weather. Her jacket doesn't look very warm either. And it looks as if it came from a secondhand shop or something. It's really dirty and hasn't got any shape. It's totally shapeless!

Listening 2

– Did you see Bill yesterday?
– No, why?
– He was going for an interview and he looked amazing!

– He'd wear jeans and a sweater to an interview!
– No, no. He was wearing this fabulous suit. You know . . . umm, three-piece suit with a waistcoat. And a deep blue tie. I've never seen him wear a tie before. And clean shoes! Sort of black business shoes. You know, the sort that businessmen wear.
– What happened?
– I don't know, but it must have cost a lot of money to buy all those clothes. And a plain white clean shirt.
– You know, I have a feeling that he really wants that job!

Listening 3

– Oh, Jane, it would be very helpful if you could meet them at the station. I'm so busy getting the food ready.
– But how will I recognise them?
– Well, they'll be wearing jeans — they always do. Both of them. You know, the faded blue type of well-worn jeans. And casual jackets. Fred usually wears a jeans jacket in faded blue just like his jeans and a T-shirt under it. His T-shirts always have something written on them. But I don't know what it'll be — he's got so many of them.
– And Kate?
– Again, a casual jacket — something sporty like a track-suit jacket. Again, I don't know what colour.
– OK, so both in jeans, Bill with jeans jacket and T-shirt, Kate with a track-suit jacket. That should be easy enough. I don't think there are going to be that many people on the train, anyway.
– Jane, that's wonderful — thanks so much.
– Not at all. See you tomorrow night.
– Thanks again. Bye.

Section 1 Reading: Design
Description of cult objects.

Section 2 Getting around
Expressing admiration for things.

Section 3 Listening
Describing clothing.

Section 4 Telephoning
Asking for travel information.

Section 5 Picture composition
Types of clothes and who might wear them.

Section 6 Discussion
Usefulness of objects.

Section 7 Letter-writing
Saying 'thank you'.

Section 8 Game
Quiz on Britain.